The Illusion of
Hopelessness

Diana,
Where there is
Life, Hope.
There is

Fran Fisher

Fran Fisher
1-15-15

Library of Congress Control Number: 2014915709

ISBN-13: 978-0-9798754-3-4

Table of Contents

Dedication

This book is dedicated to my mom and Steve, the love of my
life; to Candice and her daughters Isis and River;
to my sister, Adina.

Craig Trowhill

The Illusion of Hopelessness

Section One: The Inspiration

This book and title were inspired by
Craig Trowhill

"If I can turn my life around, so can you!"
Craig Trowhill
1973 – 2011

Vision – I AM the Courageous Warrior of Hope, the dragon slayer of illusions, powerful master of Infinite Love.

Purpose – My purpose is to break through limitations, defy disbelief, and playfully light the eternal Way.

Craig Trowhill – 2002

This book and its title were inspired by Craig Trowhill, a 36-year-old man, who was called a "game changer" by his colleagues. Craig was a martial arts instructor for youth and he was a coach for a non-profit life coaching program in Toronto, Canada, serving youth dealing with the juvenile court system.

Craig lived with an anxiety disorder and chronic physical pain. In his youth he lived the "street experience" – gangs, drugs, and violence. When he discovered martial arts and coaching, he heroically turned his life around to be of service, working with youth.

On May 21, 2011, in a dark hour of early morning, a security guard found Craig lying at the bottom of a long stairwell in a public place. The autopsy stated that he did not die as the result of any foul play or substance abuse, but from the injuries incurred by his fall down that stairwell.

Craig's death has been a great loss to the Toronto organization, the youth, the community, and his family and friends. His visionary leadership is a legacy that fuels the future generation of coaches working with youth at risk.

My Promise

Craig had a dream of publishing a book that would send a message to youth: *If I can turn my life around, so can you!* I was Craig's coach. I was so inspired by Craig's courage and determination to turn his life around and do the same for others that I had to tell his story. I declared to Craig that I was committed to helping him fulfill his vision of publishing this book. I am keeping that promise.

But there's more than keeping a promise that motivates me to carry this torch forward. One of Craig's greatest gifts to me as his coach was expanding my capacity for compassion. I now see the world differently with my heart. I used to feel powerless to make a difference. Craig showed me there is always hope. He showed me that hopelessness comes from living with fear; hope comes from looking through my compassionate heart.

I want this message to open the hearts and minds of millions of people, inspiring them to embrace the coaching approach for positive change in the lives of our youth, our communities, and ultimately for future generations. I believe this empowering approach is a key to enhancing the lives of youth with a greater sense of self, purpose, respect, and dignity.

The Title

The Illusion of Hopelessness. Craig and I had been client and coach for about six years. We were already working on this book project, but that wasn't the topic of the conversation on that particular coaching call. He had dropped into a deep, self-reflective mood and was speaking with what I called his "Zen Voice" about his passion for transforming the juvenile court system and helping youth transcend their circumstances. I heard him say the words, "the illusion of hopelessness," and that phrase took my breath away. I said, "Craig, did you hear what you just said?" He said, "No, what did I say?" I repeated, "...*the illusion of hopelessness.* That's the title of your book!" He drew in a breath and whispered, "It IS!"

I asked Craig to say more about what those words meant to him. He quoted Napoleon Hill: "*You are the master of your destiny. You can influence, direct, and control your own environment. You can make your life what you want it to be.*" And then he said, "As long as there is *life* there is *hope*, and there is always *life*, which is *love*. So there is always hope. Hopelessness is an illusion."

The Stories

The Illusion of Hopelessness shares a broad range of stories of youth, from those who are living a middle-class lifestyle with parents who can afford to pay for personal coaching to youth dealing with addictions or attention disorders to homeless youth to youth caught in domestic violence, poverty, crime, and the criminal justice system.

Contributors range from highly structured youth intervention programs with a staff of highly trained internationally certified coaches to informal approaches by individuals who have not been formally trained as coaches.

You will benefit reading these stories, if you are a:

- **Parent** of a struggling youth. You will learn effective ways of supporting your youth through their adolescent years – and beyond – or a healthy, happy, and productive life.
- **Member** of a community service organization. You will see opportunities to contribute to breaking the cycle of poverty, violence, and abuse for our youth.
- **Nonprofit** working with youth-at-risk. This book will validate your vision and mission, and inspire new models for greater effectiveness; it will provide inspiration and guidance.
- **Citizen** who is inspired to incorporate elements of the coaching approach into an existing program. You will learn tools, best practices, and resources.
- **Youth** inspired by Craig Trowhill's story. You will learn that you have within you the strengths and capacities to live true to who you are.
- **Educator or associated with Law Enforcement, Social Service, or Foster Care**. You will see how you can participate with the empowerment approach in your connections with youth.
- **Coach**. You will learn ways of applying your skills in community service.

The Situation

The future of many countries around the world may be in jeopardy because their youth are suffering from the debilitating effects of intergenerational poverty, abuse, and violence. The impact of this concerns us all, for no community is immune from the effects of a world tolerant of violence.

Youth caught up in the cycle of poverty, abuse, and violence – which often includes crime and imprisonment – face the world with hopelessness and despair. They believe that nothing can or will change for them. As with many abuse victims, they cannot conceive of any future, much less a future that offers hope for a well-lived, fulfilling life. It is expected that these young people will become adults who do not know how to value themselves or others; know little of the world beyond their own distorted experiences; and cannot conceive of peaceful, productive co-existence, supportive communities, and purposeful lives.

The Good News

We know from the experience of individuals and organizations working with youth that when young people have a safe environment they can learn to discover their unique talents, believe in their own abilities, take responsibility for their choices, trust themselves and others, and live more into their potential. An effective tool that helps generate this result is the coaching approach.

Told by those who are incorporating a coaching approach in their programs, *The Illusion of Hopelessness* shares how aspects of the coaching model are being used successfully across a range of programs for youth-at-risk.

You will learn:

- How organizations and individuals are empowering youth with hope, life skills, and resources that help them move beyond poverty, abuse, intergenerational violence, crime, and recidivism.
- How organizations and individuals can replicate this empowerment model so they can reap benefits in their own communities, such as increased productivity, community cohesion, reduced burden on taxpayers, and greater personal safety.
- How youth are benefitting from building trusting relationships and strengthening soft and hard skills working within the coaching framework, supported by trained coaches.

As a result of interviewing these contributors I now subscribe to the idea that all youth are "at-risk," by the very challenging and precarious nature of the human developmental stage they are in as they navigate from childhood to adulthood. May we, individually and collectively, find ways to build on the strength-based solutions created by these pioneers, and create a safer tomorrow for our youth.

"Where there is life, there is hope."
Stephen W. Hawking

Respectfully,
Fran Fisher
January 2015

What is Coaching?

The International Coach Federation (ICF) is the largest global association of coaches today, with approximatey 25,000 members in 80 countries (www.coachfederation.org).

The ICF adheres to a form of coaching that honors the client as the expert in his or her life and work, and that acknowledges every client as capable, creative, and resourceful. Standing on this foundation, the coach's responsibility is to:

- Discover, clarify, and align with what the client wants to achieve
- Encourage client self-discovery
- Elicit client-generated solutions and strategies
- Hold the client responsible and accountable

Coaching Behaviors that DO Support the ICF Philosophy	Behaviors that DO NOT Support the ICF philosophy
1. Asking questions	1. Telling the client what to do
2. Focusing on and championing what the client wants to achieve	2. Providing unsolicited suggestions, ideas or answers
3. Honoring confidentiality	3. Talking about the client with others; gossip
4. Providing positive feedback and acknowledgment	4. Making judgmental remarks
5. Encouraging the client to lead the conversation	5. Taking the lead or control of the conversation
6. Being a committed, focused listener	6. Not listening fully
7. Asking for clarification; trusting the client's wisdom	7. Trying to fix or quickly offering a solution
8. Allowing discomfort or silence; trust the client's capability	8. Talking to fill the silence or to avoid the discomfort
9. Expressing your opinion without attachment and allowing the other person to express theirs	9. Convincing someone to change their mind or agree with you; attached to being right
10. Making an authentic or heart to heart connection	10. Not caring or treating with respect
11. Asking permission to offer feedback or suggestions	11. Offering unsolicited feedback, ideas, or suggestions

Simply stated, coaching is a partnership of two experts. The coach is the expert of the coaching process. The client is the expert of who they are – their life and their work.

THE ICF DEFINITION OF COACHING:

Coaching is an ongoing partnership that accelerates client learning, performance, and progress in their personal and professional lives. The coach is the client's partner and champion for success.

In each session, the client chooses the focus, while the coach listens and contributes observations and questions. This interaction creates clarity and accelerates the client's progress by providing greater focus and awareness of choice. Coaching concentrates on where clients are today and what they are willing to do to get where they want to be tomorrow.

> *Coaching is the sacred space of unconditional Love,*
> *where Learning, Growth, and Transformation*
> *Naturally occur.*
> *~ Fran Fisher, Master Certified Coach*

Youth at Risk 2014

UNITED STATES OF AMERICA

In 2011 juvenile jurisdiction courts reported a total of Delinquency Offenses (personal, property, drug, public order) at 1,236,200, which was an 8% drop from 2010.

Source: National Juvenile Court Data Archive. National Center for Juvenile Justice. Pittsburgh, PA.; US Department of Justice *www.ojjdp.gov*

CANADA

Over 135,600 youths were accused of a Criminal Code offence in 2011, about 18,100 fewer than in 2010. Of those, 57 percent were "diverted" from the justice system while 43 percent were formally charged.

Source: The Macdonald Laurier Institute (MLI) commissioned *Police-reported Crime Statistics in Canada for 2013* and produced by Juristat, a division of Statistics Canada. The Juristat reports are produced in "partnership" with the Canadian Association of Chiefs of Police (CACP) and for the last number of years have resulted in media headlines announcing that "crime is down." *www.MacdonaldLaurier.ca*

ENGLAND AND WALES

Overall there were 98,837 proven offences by young people in 2012/13, down by 28 per cent from 2011/12 and down by 63 per cent since 2002/03. The largest falls in proven offences between 2009/10 and 2012/13 have been in: breach of a statutory order, which fell by 61 per cent, motoring offences by 60 per cent, and public order offences by 58 per cent. The smallest reduction has been in robbery offences, which reduced by 32 per cent between 2009/10 and 2012/13.

RE-OFFENDING BY YOUNG PEOPLE

The overall (binary) re-offending rate for young people was 35.5 per cent in 2011/12, with an average of 1.02 re-offences per offender in the cohort (frequency rate) and 2.88 re-offences per re-offender. Re-offending rates have fallen for the first time since 2007/8

Source: Youth Justice Statistics 2012/2013 for England and Wales (YJB). Youth Justice Board / Ministry of Justice, Executive Summary, Published 30th January 2014. *www.justice.gov.uk/about/yjb*

Section Two: Craig Trowhill - In His Own Words

The following are stories that Craig Trowhill shared with me by teleconference in 2009, for the purpose of laying the foundation for this book. I had already transcribed them and submitted them for his review before his untimely death in May, 2011.

~ Fran Fisher

Recorded 4-13-2009

My earliest memory of my dad is when I was about 6-7 years old. We lived in a three-story house with a basement in a nice, quiet neighborhood in Mississauga, Ontario. My dad and I were in the basement. My dad was showing me some Doppler equipment he had brought home from Vietnam. He was showing me how it works and, to me, it looked like lights and crazy lines.

Thinking it was cool looking, I had no idea what it meant or what it was for. Green screens with wavy lines. Big knobs. It was just like a big toy – a cool lit-up kind-of-thing. The wonderment I felt looking at it was never how my dad talked about it. He told me it was a very important thing, and we should be watching it all the time. I felt a sense of danger, like something was going to happen to me if I wasn't learning about what this thing was and how it worked. It was never talked about, but I felt it was about life-and-death danger if I wasn't watching this thing often.

The basement was a technical place. Lots of computers and military equipment. All sorts of weird things that I didn't really understand. It was dark, like a dungeon. This was a whole section of the basement that seemed like a totally separate part of the house, as if it just didn't belong. In the normal part of the house, there were cats, a piano, kitchen, dining room, bedroom upstairs, big TV room, and then there was this electronic crypt downstairs where my dad spent most of his time.

My dad's war experience had a very negative effect on his life. He was in the war for almost two years. He saw people die. He was in helicopters that killed people.

Many of my earliest memories involve darkness – a lot of darkness – and my dad's anger and violence. One particular incident – I'm not sure what set him off – but I do remember there was a marble statue and he knocked the head right off of it. I started crying and hid under the piano. I remember the legs very well. The pedals were medium light brown, and there were three pedals that were gold color with metal sticks going up into the piano.

The next thing I remember is being locked in a small room under the stairs in the basement. It was a low space packed with stuff so there was very little room even for a small child. The wooden door was a few centimeters thick with a metal sliding latch, and it was locked from the outside. It was dark. So dark I couldn't even see my hand in front of my face. I was fighting to get out and feeling trapped – hopeless. I remember pounding on the door, kicking it and ramming my head against it, screaming and crying, just wanting to get out. I felt no hope. Hopeless.

> I felt no hope. Hopeless.

As I feel it in my body now, I would rather have died than be in that room. To this day, I am not comfortable in pitch dark. I didn't know what else to do – only beating the door with my fist and throwing my body against it. I have no memory of how I eventually got out. It wasn't the last time I was in that room. I remember being locked in that room a few times.

My dad was big man. Very strong. When he got angry, he was a totally different person. When he sat in that basement, he was another person. He was like three different people:

basement person, rage person, the living-room-kitchen-family person.

Overall, being in that house was just like walking on egg shells. I felt scared of parts of that house and being in that house. Not just nervous scared, but terrified at times, as if I might die. All I remember is that I would run for my life from my dad when my dad got angry. It was like hell ripping open. Crazy.

I had a sense that, according to my dad, the world was a horrible place to live – that I should be ready to live or die, depending on things I didn't understand.

One thing I learned from him was that we were all going to die – it was just a matter of days or weeks. And there was no genuine happiness in life. Life was about death and horrible things that I would never be able to escape. What was going on in the world must have impacted him deeply.

My father could be completely loving and wonderful at times, but there were things he experienced in Vietnam that changed him. I look back at that time and believe that my dad sold his soul so we could live. He went to war to protect us, and it destroyed him. At the time, he believed he was doing the right thing; he knew he would pay a price for it, and he did. I love and respect him for that.

> I love and respect him for that.

Recorded 4-21-09

During grade school, my behavior outside of the home was different from what it was at home. I didn't get along with kids my age. In general, most of my peers were verbally and physically abusive toward me. I vividly remember one time in the cloakroom when one of the bullies threatened to kill me. He punched me in the face a few times and after that, I lived in fear that he would follow through on that promise.

And the bullying behavior wasn't limited to the kids. Some parents were also abusive. Today, looking back, I can understand that the kids who were the bullies likely learned that behavior at home from their parents.

But as a child, I felt so alone, scared, and there was no place that felt safe to me. I lived in my own war zone, with no one to defend me. No one taught me how to fight or stand up for myself. There was no adult or friend that I could talk to about the fear and the shame. Finally, I realized that violence was the only way to defend myself and provide some sense of safety and power – and it seemed to be the only way out of the despair and fear I felt every day.

> I realized that violence was the only way to defend myself and provide some sense of safety and power – and it seemed to be the only way out of the despair and fear I felt every day.

I learned that if I was worse than the people who were attacking me, I would be safe from them. And I was not going to wait for them to come to me anymore. If I wanted to take care of things, I had to be aggressive. My only thought was that I wanted everyone to leave me alone.

Once I started fighting back, I began to get into trouble with the Vice Principle of the school. From the Vice Principle, I learned that while violence was a solution, having a weapon was even more terrifying. The Vice Principle had a large black leather strap that he kept in his drawer. While he never used it on me, he threatened me with it. The result was that I was so terrified of that strap that I could not even think or speak. It was the same feeling I had being kept in that dark room in the basement at home.

Intimidation through violence is the easy way to attain power. Today, I feel anxious and sad when I think of an adult using their authority to control a crying child.

By this time, I was past the point of reasoning, and I certainly wasn't interested in trying to talk through problems, even if I had known how to do so. I wanted to rip my enemies apart so they wouldn't bother me again.

Things got better at home because my mom packed up, left my dad, and moved to Toronto. She knew that continuing to live with my dad was not good for my sister and me – or for her. By leaving, she abandoned everything she had, and we struggled just to make ends meet. We moved into a house next door to a funeral home. It was interesting. New house. Mom's new job in the city. I was still finishing 7th grade.

By then, of course, I had already learned to use violence to protect myself, and I had a general fear of people. It became evident that I had great difficulties adjusting to the new school and new life, so my mom took me to a psychiatrist in an effort to help me learn to adjust better.

My dad remarried right away – and that was a good thing. Keiko, the woman he married, is only about four feet tall, Japanese, born in an internment camp, and she was a real tough cookie. She loved me, and we are still very close today. Her son eventually became like my brother.

When my sister and I went to see him on the weekends, my dad was still very angry and aggressive. One day he was furious at us and we hid in the bathroom. He came after us and smashed the door down. We ran past him and down into the basement. Keiko looked my dad in the face and said, "If you touch this kid, I will kill you." She had had enough. She was going to kick his ass. Dad just backed off and went upstairs.

My mom and Keiko – I am grateful for these two women in my life. Their efforts and their love for me helped saved me from further abuse from my father. Some people think women are not powerful, but I think the exact opposite. I don't know what would have happened if those two women hadn't protected and defended me.

17

Recorded 4-27-09

When we moved to Toronto, my sister started hanging out with a group of kids who were just as abusive as the ones I had left behind. It seemed that I just kept falling into that. Most kids think that there is something wrong with them when they continually face this kind of abuse. I certainly did.

I was learning to be more violent because I had to survive among these violent people. I got into shoplifting and then robbing people, mostly for money. I was quickly learning negative life skills. I also started drinking a lot and smoking drugs. This was just before going into high school.

It seemed that those years were marked mostly by the fights I had, and the violence I was the recipient of or that I initiated. I became bolder at robbing others, and more violent toward others. The drugs and alcohol fueled my behavior. By now, my behavior at home mirrored who I had become on the streets, severely impacting my relationship with my mom and sister. I believed that I was evil, that my sole purpose in life was to either suffer myself or create suffering for others, and I was done being the victim. I much preferred inflicting suffering on others. All I could feel was anger and hate toward others and myself. I thought there was something wrong with me, and nothing could be done to change that.

I remember a particularly bad fight over a girl. I beat the guy up, stabbed him in the leg, and hit him in the head with a frying pan. He was hurt pretty bad, but he managed to get out on his own.

In an effort to change my escalating bad behavior, my mother sent me to an alternative school. I was afraid of every one there, and by then my preferred coping skills were to be aggressive and violent.

It had become evident to my mom that I was having difficulty adjusting to the new school and new life, so she took me to a psychiatrist in an effort to help me learn to adjust. The psychiatrist diagnosed that I had a slight obsessive compulsive disorder, a panic disorder, and depression.

I practiced boxing and martial arts and lifted weights in my room. I started carrying weapons so I felt safer. I wore hip chains, heavy link chains with pad locks tied to the end, and steel-toed boots. I carried sticks from martial arts and anything else I could use as a weapon.

Then I went to another new school for my high school years. I hung out with a crowd of kids who were just like me, but I had no real friends. Most people I met were afraid of me, and that was okay with me. My philosophy was that the best defense was a good offense. At least I wasn't being bullied or ridiculed. I had a reputation as a violent outcast who carried a lot of weapons. It was about this same time that I started selling drugs.

My high school years were filled with doing just enough schoolwork to get by, skipping classes, selling drugs during school, collecting the money, and beating up people. People were so scared they didn't try to involve the police. I had a very bad reputation – people thought I was crazy – and I was proud of that reputation. Everybody knew my name and knew to stay out of my way. The people I associated with were just as bad or worse than I was. Some of them carried guns, although I never did. I preferred more personal types of weapons, like knives.

Eventually, I graduated from high school with the aid of several persistent teachers who, for some reason I never understood, really believed in me. Perhaps they saw that

> They saw something in me that I never saw in myself.

when I did apply myself, I did well. They saw something in me that I never saw in myself. Today, I am thankful for their support, although I would never have shown it then.

Then I became a member of a gang organized around drugs and violence. We were called the Cuba Posse because we wore lapel pins of Cuba from a travel agency. We were well known all over the city.

A rival gang threatened to kidnap and kill me. In retaliation for that threat, we broke into the leader's home in the middle of the night, taped him to a chair, beat him up, held knives to his throat, and told him that he was going to die if he didn't stop the threats. It must have worked because we weren't threatened by that gang again.

I was consumed by the violence and the gang life. I felt so much rage and hate, which covered up the fear that I wouldn't allow myself to feel. I could never trust anyone, not even the people I hung out with. I embraced these behaviors and attitudes as my only choice in how to live, and it contaminated every part of my life. By the time I was 18, I had been arrested for fighting, dealing with a bully.

About this time, my grandfather died unexpectedly of a heart attack. During this time, my mother's sister also lived with us for two years while she was slowly dying of cancer. These circumstances were financially and emotionally challenging for my mother. She was grieving the loss of her father and the slow, painful loss of her sister. I'm sure she was devastated by my behavior as well, even though I stayed away from home a considerable amount of time. I thought I was helping by staying out of her way. I know my mom worked hard to keep food on the table and a roof over our heads, but I was so consumed by my own problems that it was impossible for me to consider the feelings of others, even family. There were times when the violence that surrounded me spilled over into our home life, and I know that my mother and sister were both traumatized by it.

There were other deaths during this period of my life. Not only did family members die, but a favorite teacher died, and a couple of kids I knew committed suicide. These deaths also colored my perspective on life and deepened my belief that I had no control over what happened to me – more hopelessness. I hated the universe and everyone in it. I made myself believe that I didn't care about anything. The universe and I were at war, and it was this war that kept me engaged and alive.

Drugs were a huge part of my life then. I smoked everything – weed, hash, acid, mushrooms, PCP. Because I was scared that I would contract AIDS, I never did heroin or crack or injected drugs. At least I was discriminating about the drugs, although I hated to acknowledge that it was fear that made me draw the line.

I sold marijuana, cocaine, and lots of acid – anything I could get my hands on. For me, it wasn't about making money. It was just about me getting my own drugs. Other kids bought cars and other stuff with their money, but I was in business to make only enough money to buy my own drugs.

The police knew who we were. We got away with a lot of illegal activities without getting caught. Most of our crimes were to get money to buy drugs. However, there were times when we'd get arrested. I'd been arrested enough to know the routine: get arrested, get processed, go to court, and try to get out of spending any time in jail.

Fortunately, I served no major jail time. I always got out. When you are in custody, all you learn is how to be a better criminal. Even in those circumstances, my style benefitted me to some extent because I knew how to connect to people, and I was big and strong, so I was able to hold my own if anyone gave me any trouble.

This way of life continued until I was about 21. Then, I started to notice the impact I was having on those around me, and the circumstances in which I found myself. I began to develop a conscience and had a hard time dealing with what I had done and what I was doing. My lifestyle changed dramatically, and it started by not leaving the house. For almost three years, I rarely went outside my home.

I was 21 and I didn't have a job or any skills with which to earn money other than dealing drugs or victimizing others. I noticed that I couldn't tolerate being outside or around people. I started to look at what I had done in my life. My recurring thought was, "Oh, my God, what have I done?"

I was depressed. Sometime during this period, I stopped believing that I was meant to be evil, so I was deeply conflicted with the good side of me that was coming out. I started lifting weights a lot in an effort to relieve the anxiety I felt. Then I injured my shoulder and I couldn't lift weights for at least a year. This lack of physical activity meant that I was truly left alone with my thoughts and myself. I reflected on who I had been, and I started thinking about all the people I had victimized. I didn't want to be that person anymore.

> I didn't want to be that person anymore.

I began defying my belief that my whole life had been a mistake. I didn't want to see anyone get hurt or die anymore. I was tired of people chasing me in my dreams. In desperation, I knew I had to get out of the house. Something inside of me told me to check out the martial arts school near my home.

Master Joe ran the martial arts school. I talked to him for four solid hours, telling him my whole life story. I told him I didn't want it anymore. I cried my eyes out and asked him to help me. And he did.

I learned a lot about how to live life through studying martial arts with Master Joe. I now say to anyone I hurt, "I am sorry." No excuses. I really am sorry. Today, I feel ashamed of who I was and what I did at that time in my life, and I do not like to talk about it. I feel horrible about the things I did. I still think about some of the people I hurt. I remember the look in their eyes when I hurt them. I imagine that there are people I have hurt who have not forgotten or will ever forgive me. I know that I cannot forget the pain I caused. Even though I was harmed by others, I have learned to accept it so that I can be at peace, but I still have a very difficult time forgiving myself about what I've done to others and accepting the poor choices I made.

Through practicing martial arts, I started to understand that how I live life is a choice – my choice. I can never change what happened in the past, but I can change how I deal with the things that happened. I can now choose understanding, compassion, and forgiveness for all the others and myself.

> I can now choose understanding, compassion, and forgiveness for all the others and myself.

Recorded 5-11-09

I had been around martial arts since I was 8, so I wasn't totally new to the concepts. When I started training in Hap Kido, I started doing it three hours a day, seven days a week. That took me away from the things I had been doing that were causing me so much angst. It gave me something positive to focus on.

I grew obsessed with learning the techniques and tactics. Over the following seven years, I was privileged to work with one of the most gifted instructors, Grand Master Park, and acquired a great deal of master training, including police security forces training. Now, instead of being consumed with rage and violence, I was completely obsessed with achieving a master's rank in martial arts. I also started teaching kids' classes, and eventually started running the school under Master Joe's supervision.

Even though I was still dealing with the anxiety disorder and still trying to figure out how to function around people in my life, my attitudes and my perspective began to change as I progressed in martial arts. I was introduced to their strong

23

code of ethics. I learned to be respectful of others and myself. Rudeness was not allowed. I learned to respond with "Yes, ma'am. No, sir." No slack, no excuses. I was learning how to relate to others with courtesy and respect. I realized that I was very good at what I did, which instilled a sense of accomplishment and confidence that I had never felt before. And, I felt respect and admiration from others for how I was *being*. I learned that others either liked or at least respected me, and I didn't have to command their respect (or what I had come to believe was respect) through violence and intimidation. I am enormously grateful to those black belts and Master Joe who taught me so much. They helped me learn how to be in relationships with other people and how to be in relationship with myself in ways I never thought possible. These experiences marked the beginning of enormous changes in my life – from the inside out. Quite a change for someone who never thought he would live to see his 23rd birthday.

About that time, I met a woman named Kate Sharp through my martial arts work with kids. I don't remember how, exactly. She invited me to work with her in a program she was running, sponsored by the Toronto District School Board. This experience boosted my self-confidence.

The positive changes in my life were highly encouraging to those closest to me, especially my mother. To encourage my continued positive transformation, my mother offered to support me so that I could attend Chef's School. I dropped out. Next was Management School. I dropped out of that. I tried a Fitness Trainer course. I dropped it. It seemed that the only thing I could succeed at was martial arts. I knew how to fight and to move. That was all I knew about myself and my skills and talents. Not much to build a life on – I also knew that. But, I didn't know how to do anything more – or how to find out what I was good at and how I could support myself. I felt hopeless about my ability to have a life that meant something. I didn't – wouldn't – go back to the violence and anger, but what else existed out there in the world for me? I had tried so many things and always came away feeling like a failure.

During the time that we lived in Toronto, my mother had become a certified coach. When she left my father and we moved to Toronto, she decided to study psychology. While she was working on her Ph.D., her sister came to live with us. It was very hard on all of us because her sister was dying of brain cancer. Mom realized that she needed to leave graduate school and find a career that would make enough money to support all of us. She took a job at Bayview Cancer Clinic as a psychologist, which put her in contact with a variety of individuals and organizations. As a result of her work at the clinic, she received an offer to coach a corporate management team, which she accepted because it would bring in a lot more money. Her experience working with that management team led her to becoming a certified coach.

Finally, in 2002, my mother suggested that I consider becoming a life coach, which was her profession. She had seen me fail over and over, but she continued to believe in me – she knew it was just a matter of finding the right match for my skills, personality, and interests. She also knew I needed to be challenged in ways that would help me grow personally, just as I'd done in martial arts. We had never really discussed her work before – I thought it was kind of like counseling, and I certainly didn't want to go there – but also because it was confidential in nature, and I'd never really been interested in finding out more.

As encouragement, Mom explained coaching to me as a new way of learning how to *be* authentically oneself and how to *be and work* with others. She also encouraged me to check it out because she saw a gift in me – a gift of being able to see what other people need. I still had great anxiety and awkwardness in relating to others, and I had very little insight into who I really was or what I might be capable of – a *real me* that was *not* defined solely by my physical abilities or my former violent history. I was intrigued by this new concept that seemed somewhat aligned with the respectfulness I'd learned in martial arts. When Mom encouraged me to look into coaching skills training, I agreed.

I took the *Introduction to Coaching* class and I was hooked. There was an entire certification program of coaching skills training that I could take that would provide me with a professional certificate so that I could then work with others. To me, getting a certificate was like graduating from college with a four-year degree! I then made an important decision. I decided to take all of the coursework in Seattle, Washington, where there was a well-established coaching school owned by a friend of my mother's. Intuitively, it seemed safer for me to explore this new avenue far away from people who knew the "old" me, even though it was a huge challenge for me to overcome my fear of flying from Toronto to Seattle.

I attended four weekend workshops over a period of eight months. The coach training was challenging. At the same time, I felt myself shifting and opening up to new ideas and ways of being that felt far more authentic than anything I'd ever tried, with the exception of martial arts. The philosophy made sense to me. Through coach training, I learned to listen, ask thought-provoking questions, and offer intuitive insights. It was a process that really made sense to me. It felt very much like what I did in martial arts. I felt like I was doing something that I already knew how to do and that I was just remembering it. It felt so natural it even freaked me out a bit. My resistance made the work harder than it needed to be, due to my awe at the simplicity and effectiveness of the program. I still believed that life and work should be hard! It never occurred to me that talents and gifts usually show up as being easy and natural – and authentically personal.

It was the Living Your Vision® experience in the coach training that was life-changing for me! This was a powerful process where each trainee took time to reflect on who they are and their purpose in life. In my small group, we helped each other identify words and meanings that truly stated the essence of each of us. We took turns being in the center of a small circle so we could focus 100% of our energy on serving the person in the center, helping that person find their authentic "I AM" statement that expressed their essence and purpose.

When it was my turn, I was so uncomfortable I wanted to bolt. But then I surrendered to the process, let down my defenses, and allowed myself to feel the love, safety, and support of my teammates. My team helped me get underneath all my negative judgments about myself and my fears, and shame, and anxiety to find the exact words that truly expressed the Core Truth of my being. My supporters in the process wouldn't let me settle for less. It was a big freakin' deal to let myself be supported and encouraged to let the real me out!

When I found the words that felt the most inspiring, authentic, and meaningful for me – as a statement of who I am – I felt a huge shift in my energy and my relationship with myself and the world. I felt it down to my very core, and I was amazed that I could actually own this statement about me as my truth. Every single word has deep metaphorical meaning for me. My "I AM" statement has been transformational for me.

I Am the Courageous Warrior of hope, the dragon slayer of illusions, powerful master of Infinite Love. My Life Purpose is to break through limitations, defy disbelief, and playfully light the Eternal Way.

Identifying my purpose in life has made a huge difference for me. Now, when I doubt myself or my anxiety pulls me off center, I say it to myself out loud, and I feel myself reconnecting with my authentic power. I don't just feel these words in my heart and mind. I feel them in my body, too. *THIS* is who I am. *THIS* is my destiny. THIS is what I was born for.

I am proud to say that I graduated from coach training with honors. I knew I made a positive impact when I worked with others. I realized that I could make a different kind of impact in the world, and I really enjoyed it! I was now exercising my intellect and intuition while connecting on a close, personal level with others. Quite a new experience for me!

My experience is that martial arts and coaching are very similar in that they are both about the flow of energy, connection with self and others, and finding one's way of being in the world. I had already learned that the energy between two people had a lot to do with the body. Techniques in martial arts taught me experientially about feeling the energy flow in my body and connecting with the energy of another person. Now I was developing a deep connection to something deeper that supported my process. It was more about energy than technique, and I believed that I was learning how the world actually works. It was about how relationships work. How we all function. How we all live. How we all interact. How we are all connected to each other.

In 2004, about the time I started attaining some sense of stability in my life, I experienced a devastating loss. That was the year my friend Sean died. Sean was one of my very closest friends from high school. He knew everything about me. We talked every day.

Sean was severely injured in a fire at his home. He was burned over 95% of his body, but he managed to save his family. Sean was taken to the hospital; mercifully, he was in a coma. I went into the hospital to see him. It was very hard for me to see Sean because the person I knew was no longer there. One month later his family elected to take him off life support because he was brain dead. He was gone. The loss hurt more than anything I had ever experienced, and I cried more than I believed I could. Because of all the work I had done in martial arts and coach training, I was no longer frozen emotionally, and the pain of Sean's death brought me to my knees. I spoke at his funeral. It all seemed to happen so quickly. At 27, my best friend died. He was just gone. Life over. And he had wanted to do so much. He was a beautiful person.

Then, another friend died in a chemical fire on his job. The next year, another kid we knew from high school was stabbed to death in the streets of Toronto. As hard as I had worked to change my life, I was terribly impacted by these events. A lot of my friends were, too. They fell victim to drug abuse and addiction. Some just disappeared. It seemed that, once again, violence and death were all around me. I had thought that bad part of my life was over, but it was still happening. From the choices I had made, it could have been me.

I looked at the impact those deaths had on others. Many lives were devastated by those deaths. That gave me more resolve not to do harm. I felt my old anger coming back, and I felt so helpless to stop it. Life was too fucking short.

I still shut down. I closed myself off. I could feel myself plummeting again into depression and hopelessness. But for the first time, I realized what was happening, so I took action to support myself. The anger and sadness I felt helped me get very clear. The only way I wanted to impact people was in a positive way.

Recorded 5-18-09

Because I enjoyed doing martial arts with Kate Sharp's program, I applied for and received permission from the Toronto district school board to conduct martial arts programs in the elementary schools. I also began doing some coaching.

In the past, whenever my mom would say, "Trust the Universe," I would say "Fuck the Universe." Now I chose to be supported by the Universe. I felt like the Universe was supporting my efforts, which in turn increased my confidence in choosing coaching.

I believe Universal Energy equates to God, which is the conscious energy all around us. Through experiencing different types of energy in martial arts, I came to believe that there was much more in the world than just what I could see. I felt that there was a conscious, living energy that supported me. I started to play with that idea and test it to see what would happen.

I started asking questions of my "Conscious Self." I would ask a question in my head and then paid specific attention to the words of a song or an ad that caught my attention and particularly resonated with me. Most of my questions were about my life purpose: "How do I move forward?" or "How do I deal with this situation?" I would get answers that seemed intuitively right for me. The more I practiced, the more I got answers – positive answers – and always something very specific and affirming. These "experiments" led me to believe that something in the Universe had my best interests in mind. I felt as if I was having a conversation with the Universe. There was either a consciousness out there or I was going insane! As I practiced this, the more specific and immediate the answers came.

Once I was walking through the hallway feeling overwhelmed by what was going in my life. I was thinking, "What is this all about? I don't know what to do." I looked up and saw the gym sign on the wall that said "Good Life." I have walked by that sign in my hallway a thousand times, but this time it spoke to me. It answered my question.

The more I focused on the positive, the more positive answers would come. I trusted that inner voice and it gave me the right answers. It is a very different feeling thinking that the Universe is supporting me, and it's a very different feeling from being supported by family and friends. It made me feel like my life had a purpose above and beyond what I had known – a grand design. Even though I have choices, there is a big plan.

This growing awareness and receiving answers to my questions about life, my life, and the actions to take, was extremely humbling, and I really appreciated it. Those answers were like an acknowledgment that my path is important, and I could ask for help and receive it from my Conscious Self and the Universe.

I have come to believe that everybody is unique and equally important – that everything happens for a reason. Life is a balance of good and evil, light and dark, and everyone has their own unique perspective about every situation.

This connection with my Conscious Self and the Universe has been incredibly powerful for me. While the answers are not always answers I wanted to hear, there were always answers, and they were always true for me.

Once I was sitting in my living room thinking about my past, thinking about who I am being now, feeling so many emotions about my life – and why did it have to be that way? "Why did I end up doing this work?" "What does this mean?" "How am I supposed to live like this?" The answer came when I was watching a movie called *Identity*. The word "identity" stuck out for me, and I focused on that word and what it meant. Who I am is my identity and, as good or as bad as it has been, it is the unchangeable of who I am. It is very empowering to consider that who I am choosing to be at any moment continues to shape my identity. This helps me understand who I am today and that I can shape who I am to become. This self-acceptance has made a huge difference in how I view myself and how I experience others.

Now I am working with young offenders in the PACT organization. In coaching young offenders, I've asked myself, "Why do I work with these kids? They are little hell raisers like I was." "Why am I here?" "How do I survive this?" "Why is this happening?" I love the work because it is challenging, and my life experience has brought me to this place. I have something to offer these young people who are so much like I was at their age.

When I was young, I would have given anything to have someone respect me enough to just listen to me without judgment – not telling me what to do – but to help me understand the impact of my choices. That is what I try to do today with the young offenders I work with. That is why I choose to work with these young adults.

> When I was young, I would have given anything to have someone respect me enough to just listen to me without judgment – not telling me what to do – but to help me understand the impact of my choices. That is what I try to do today with the young offenders I work with.

Generally, the kids are on charges because of crimes they have committed and are entrenched in the court system. They feel hopeless. Lots of them have been victims of abuse and their lives are difficult. I can't fix them, but I can offer my experiences and help empower them through my coaching skills and caring about what happens to them. At the same time, it's important that I remain somewhat detached so I can be more objective.

Seeing these young people engaged in the coaching process – which is helping them discover who they are, identify the choices they have, and see how their actions and emotions have a strong impact on themselves and others – is a big way that I can give back.

Sometimes I feel guilty about all the bad things I've done, but today I choose to do only good – to be a positive influence – and I feel very good about that. Maybe it will make amends for what I've done in the past, and this work gives my life purpose.

So, why am I doing this kind of work? If one person reads my story and finds a sense of hope for their own life to change – if my story helps just one person – it will be worth it.

I am grateful today. I appreciate the process and probably wouldn't change any of it. It has shaped me into who I am today. I have great empathy for others. I know pain. I know suffering, but after all that has happened, I am left with gratitude.

I now believe everything happens for a reason. Everybody is unique and equally important. Life is a balance of good and evil, light and dark, and everyone has their own unique perspective about every situation. The Universe is love, not hate, and that love has carried me. It is love and supportiveness and peace.

MORNING SONG

Hello there, Universe, what do you say?
What are the lessons for me today?
I know you'll support me in finding my way
But first there are some things that I'd like to say.

I struggle sometimes with the choices I have
Sometimes I cry, and sometimes I'm sad
But hearing you sing makes me so glad
You're my brother, my sister, my Mom, and my Dad.

So let's start the journey with a smile and a grin
Challenge perspectives that you'll put me in
No matter the task, I know I can win
I'm ready now Universe... Let the learning begin.

~ Craig Trowhill

Section Three: PACT

David Lockett

Interviewed by Fran Fisher, July 25, 2012

David Lockett is Co-Founder and President of the PACT Urban Peace Program, Toronto, Ontario, Canada. David has volunteered half of his working career to create and run two charities involved in preventing violence in our society and nurturing the potential in troubled youth. Over 15,000 people have benefited from these two charities. In 1987 David became a charter member of the Parkdale High Park Rotary club, and in 2010 David was one of a hundred Canadians nominated by the Globe and Mail as a Transformational Canadian. PACT (Participation, Acknowledgment, Commitment, Transformation) has been acknowledged by the United Nations for its work and was awarded the Rotary Urban Peace Award.

http://pactprogram.ca/
djlockett@rogers.com
(416) 256-0726

Fran: What was your original inspiration for the PACT program?

David: It started when I realized that shelters really deal with the effects of domestic violence and behavior. To create a meaningful solution to the problem would have to involve a new way of looking at things. The idea was to develop a program that would help support, improve, and correct the underlying behavior that is really intergenerational, in many ways, that affects and drives violence in the home environment. In many cases that same negative environment self-perpetuates. The idea was to build a program.

Fran: So the inspiration was shifting from a system reacting to the effects to getting at the underlying cause and then having an impact on shifting the underlying cause. Right?

David: Exactly.

Fran: Tell me about how you got the program launched.

David: In 1993, I decided to pursue this vision of creating a charity that dealt with the underlying cause of domestic violence. I formed the original board. The idea started to self-perpetuate when we decided to take a fresh look. We really didn't have a lot of experience in the area. I did all of three years of research about what worked and what didn't work. We decided that we were going to look everywhere to discover programs that were effective, and model the principles that made them effective. So it almost became a modeling project.

The first program we modeled was a victim offender mediation program that started in Australia. It was a pre-charge diversion program that was really effective for diverting less serious crime. It was a mediation program that encompassed victims and offenders, and it was court referred. It became an alternative type of process to the normal courts. The idea was to not formally charge, but giving the offender a second chance. A policeman and a criminal lawyer started the program in a little town in British Columbia, and it really worked. I saw an article about it in *Reader's Digest*. I called them up and asked them to come to Toronto. I called the Toronto Superintendent of Police, Bill Blair, and he agreed to give it a shot. That was around 12 years ago.

We got some diversions from the police force and local Assistant Crown Attorney Rick Blouin, from a youth group that was involved. Our work with them was successful. We went on for the next ten years to at least 2,000 court-referred mediations that involved victims and offenders, in different areas in the Greater Toronto Area. That was the first platform of PACT, which was basically pre-charge diversion and mediation.

Fran: What an incredible impact. To hear your story it sounds like this was an idea whose "time has come."

David: It's interesting that, as an organization, one of the things you find if you talk to other successful organizations – one thing that Founders will tell you – is that in going through this process you have to be extremely firm to stick to the values behind your vision. In our case, it was to break the cycle and also develop programs to bring out the potential. When youths get caught in the system and they are having problems in the education systems, they are not going to live up to their potential. So having a highly effective experiential-based skill development program available in the community is certainly a way to get them deferred through court referrals or community service orders. It was a really great way to deal with that segment of our youth population that is involved with the courts who are not criminals, but are having problems with the educational system and could fall into that trap of poverty and welfare and not live up to their potential.

That's one aspect. The other aspect is getting back to our core issue and that vision to break the intergenerational cycle of violence. It was about that time that I learned about a Nobel Prize winner for Chemistry, awarded at the University of Toronto, a Canadian physicist named John Polanyi (*http://www.utoronto.ca/jpolanyi*). Polanyi wrote a paper about how in science and in architecture, form follows function, and that if, as a society, we can really take a close look, we can discover what the problems are without trying to adapt them to ineffective government program models. This was profound for me to discover the core simplicity of the problem and then begin to develop meaningful solutions that eloquently meet the needs. Then we can really eliminate 95%

of the programs that don't work and create situations that will truly make highly effective, meaningful solutions. John Polanyi called that "form following function." He shaped a paper around that, and he sent it back to Sweden to the Nobel Laureate committee and they thought it was so profound that

> This was profound for me to discover the core simplicity of the problem and then begin to develop meaningful solutions that eloquently meet the needs.

they circulated it to pretty much every government in the world. The idea was that here, right in front of us, lies a solution to create a renaissance if we could allow the community and the talent within the community – which is kind of what we have done with PACT – to truly have access at an operational level a way to fix social problems.

You know, we can truly transform the world. If you look at our LifePlan Coaching Program, and look at our blueprint for social change, and our organizing principles, one of the fundamental organizing principles is "form follows function." It's a life of service and doing things unconditionally without agenda or being involved in a bureaucratic perspective. As a community member, it gives you the opportunity to identify those simple needs and to integrate simple solutions in the way that form follows function.

Fran: How is "form follows function" demonstrated in the design of your program?

David: The most eloquent example is our LifePlan Coaching Program. It's a service with a great vision for breaking inter-generational cycles, and it takes this extremely complicated problem on, with one very simple and powerful solution. We did the research, and we found that the vast majority of crime is caused by a

> That small fraction of our society is responsible for the vast majority of the crimes.

fractional few, and these fractional few individuals are born in a negative family environment. A percentage of them became extremely habitual and violent and that small fraction of our society is responsible for the vast majority of the crimes. But what we do as a society is that we create these ineffective programs and do an ineffective job with the kids that are not habitual criminals who need support to get an education. We spend billions not solving the problem. So what LifePlan basically does is it targets those kids. It truly meets the needs of a kid who comes from that background and takes them out of an environment like jail and begins to rebuild their lives, giving them all the normal things that normal kids have. It gives them access to the resources they need to make a goal, to get to a normal life, and the majority of the youth have.

I'm not saying that there are not dysfunctional families, but I'm saying there is a big difference between a kid that's in jail at 15 and a kid that has problems coming from a good family. But you take kids from the projects that don't have a father, who come from poor backgrounds and are living in the most negative environments, that's where all the problems come from. In our LifePlan Coaching Program, 60% of the kids are seeing incredible progress. That is an example of one simple program of coaching. The adaptation of that model is doing something that nobody has ever done.

Fran: It's working. Your results are certainly validating this theory, aren't they?

David: Absolutely! It's not only where have we come from, but it's where we can go. About $5–7,000 [CAD] covers the cost of coaching a youth in the PACT Program – turning the life of a youth around. For every youth that breaks the cycle, we save society at least two million dollars, so the leveraging and power of this investment is absolutely remarkable. You can talk about the dynamics of the money all you want, but yesterday in Toronto we had the most violent incident occur in the history of the city. It happened on Sunday night in one of the most difficult areas of the city, with lots of projects. There was a neighborhood welcome party with about 200 people there. A couple of gangs showed up, got into a fight, fired an automatic weapon, and 22 people were shot. Two people were killed – a 14-year-old and a 19-year-old. It is the worst violent incident in the history of this city, and the reason I'm bringing that up is because I could talk to you about saving countless lives and billions of dollars. When we start to factor in the cost of victimization, can you imagine? 22 people were shot, a middle class family lost a 14-year-old daughter, and a young man who just graduated from a university is dead, just because they were at a party and someone there had a gun and opened fire in the crowd. So my question is, what would have happened if that kid had come to PACT when he was 13? What would happen if our organization had five million dollars?

Our next step is to leverage our Toronto school partnership and integrate and adapt our coaching model. That's the power of this concept. I thought about it yesterday and, of course, it's been all over the Canadian media. It's been all over international media, and it's the same bullshit. No one is really talking about the problem. The problem is that there is a kid who's at risk that has been charged in the court a couple of times, who goes out and grabs a gun and starts shooting people in a crowd. This is a habitual criminal, right? We've got to get to them early and, by doing that, we can build peace anywhere in the world. It's the same universal principle or law.

Fran: Yes, exactly! It just breaks your heart, doesn't it, David?

David: Oh yeah, and what I find so profound about it is that we're 18 years into this, and we have the endorsement from the Chief Justice System down. We are funded. We've got benchmark results. The community has to change, and we're in the position to change with it. It's a teachable process. So we want to take our skill involvement programs and let them

> The "crown jewel" is this power for social change, which is driven by the power behind the coaching.

unfold so they get bigger, and they become examples by taking a gang-banger down a different path. The "crown jewel" is this power for social change, which is driven by the power behind the coaching. I'm not a coach. I'm just the guy that said the coaching thing seems to make a lot of sense, and I understand the problems.

Fran: Yes, you are the visionary with a passion for influencing profound change in our communities. Let's talk about PACT some more. What does PACT stand for?

David: The story behind that goes back 19 years. A whole team of people helped us design the name. We came up with PACT, which stands for **Participation, Acknowledgment, Commitment, and Transformation**. Those are the four stages a youth goes through in order to transform his life. From an internal perspective, it is a decision that a youth will go through because it all comes down to choice. On a macro perspective, it's the same choice a community can make. It's those four fundamentals of making a decision to *Participate, Acknowledge* that we really have a problem, and making a *Commitment* to do whatever it takes to make that *Transformation* in the society. So, it as much applicable to an *individual* who wants a change as it is to a *community* that wants a change.

We built a system that is massively cost effective and highly effective and, if we're given the money, which I'm sure we will attract, we will create a program for sharing and modeling on a "pilot" basis. The ultimate goal is to perfect and teach the model to others, from funding to program delivery. That's how we will deliver it to a million people. It can be a great thing for coaches because coaches want to make a living at what they do, and they want to have a positive impact on the lives of those they coach.

It has become apparent that a life coach can play a major role in any individual having a challenge in the social infrastructures. The model simply works when you can take an individual outside the system to help rebuild their lives.

Fran: What is your short-term goal; say in the next year?

David: I intend to raise about a million and a half dollars in the next eight months and expand the program to 50 kids a year. Then I want to create an international fund to see more coaching start up in other areas; hopefully, with the support of Rotary International.

Fran: Well, that's what it's going to take – a network of support, right?

David: Yes. I see people coming from all over the world to learn the process here, either online or in person. On some levels, that's already happening; we have more international coaches, teams, and observers coming to PACT every year now.

There is another thing I want to share with you, Fran, that I think would really touch you. A couple of years ago I was doing some work on some micro-fundraising models, and I was getting a lot of perspective from Craig at the time. I saved some of his emails, just to refer back to, and I wanted to read you a few excerpts regarding our LifePlan Coaching Program. This would have been in April 2009, and this was about the big picture to teach it everywhere. I presented this vision to him, and this is what he said to me:

(Craig Trowhill): Okay, David. I read the vision and I started to cry. Between you and me, I have known this kid you are talking about since high school. First off, he was young so we looked after him, but as Alex got older, he started to get into drug dealing, cocaine actually. Alex had just got his real estate license, and he had the world at his door, but instead he decided to get involved with drugs and dealing because the money was good, and he was not going to do it forever. I tried

to get him out of it. I talked to him many times about stopping. In 2005, Alex was stabbed repeatedly over a drug deal. He was dumped in an ally, where he died. He died slowly and alone in that ally.

Of course his parents and his brother were devastated by these events. I have seen many die in my life. The glamorous criminal life is an illusion. I have lived it and survived, but I am one in hundreds that fall into the jail of death because of a criminal lifestyle. I will live with these horrible memories until I die....

The impact of youth falling into crime is huge. Alex's death affected hundreds of people, like the butterfly effect. Every small crime affects us all. We are not separate from the youth. Everything they choose to do affects us all. I hope you truly consider me in helping with fundraising. I don't know how I can help. I do know I am supposed to be here. To take my knowledge from climbing my way back up – to let the world know that it can be done.

Fran: It's so sad he is not here today to help you with your fundraising.

David: That guy inspired me. He was just a star, you know. He was a warrior – that's the best way to describe Craig. I have been in the business for 38 years, and I ran PACT and have been involved with Rotary for 28 years. I meet tons of people, and he is one of those guys I have seen in my travels that had the most integrity because what you saw was exactly what you got.

Fran: Yes, that is so true from my experience of him as well. It said in your website video that Craig was a "game changer." What did that mean? How did that look?

David: Craig seemed to be getting better results than the other coaches, and he was dealing with some of the more challenging cases. I asked him, "What are you doing that's different?" He said, "Oh, you know, I like to hang around, play video games, and get to know them for the first couple of months." He was able to establish trust with these kids and be able to see where they were at, and that is what separated him. Once he had their trust, he was able to help them make changes in their lives. So I think it was his courage and his ability to enter their world. Based on that important rapport-building component, I made the official decision that with any case, I'm willing to extend coaching up to a year and a half. The reason is because if it takes three or four months to get some kids to trust, then it's after that point the real coaching begins, right?

Fran: Yes, and that leads to my next question. What did you learn that inspired changes in the program over time?

David: The first thing we learned is how important it is to bring in coaches that have the natural ability to develop rapport. Also, that we needed structure and continuity among the coaches. So, we identified six key strategies or tools that we use to train and enact and, at an operational level, make sure they are being followed. The strategies we came up with are:

(1) Wheel of life
(2) Goal setting through strength
(3) Establishing key values
(4) Taking action
(5) Developing rapport
(6) Outcomes

These are the things we want to see happening in every coaching relationship. We are starting to see that these tools work. You're a coach, Fran. I don't have to tell you that there is nothing more powerful than looking at the Wheel of Life, right? Particularly when you can relate your life to what the wheel looks like when you have rated yourself in all those areas.

Fran: Absolutely! It's a very powerful awareness-building tool. What have been your challenges growing this program?

David: Just the notion of formulating a program that has checks and balances – from intake to reporting and marketing – it takes a lot of time. So, we find ourselves in uncharted waters because of all these dynamics that had to come together, a lot of which has taken time. We find ourselves in this unique position where we're on the crest of the wave, and no one else is really on it. Then, we look at the results we're getting, and we look at how far we've come, and then we say, "How much farther can we go?" We really have a remarkable opportunity. The game changer was not just who Craig was – the coaching model is the game changer.

> The coaching model is the game changer.

Fran: Yes, well said.

David: Another key change is our intake process. We learned that we have to feel if a kid is ready to go. We can't get them to change unless they want to change, you know? So about a year ago, we started a five-week intake program. We put them into the system and wait until we see a commitment. We get them to sign a contract. Our rule is that if you miss three meetings, you have to go, unless you have a very good excuse. Basically, we screen them. Rather than just saying we'll take them into a program and having them fail, what we do is almost like a test. The intake process is to make sure there is going to be that spark. About half way into the intake process, if we see something that's an improvement, then we go with it.

It's hard to change people who don't want to change. It's important to say that we all need a vision for our life, and you need to immerse people in environments where they can learn to become compassionate for themselves and others. I see that with our skill development programs. That's another development in our program that is a key to our success.

You know Akeem Richardson (*real name, by permission*), Craig's former client, the kid that's in our film? He definitely isn't living up to his potential in life, and part of that difficulty is having that whole back path. What we're trying to achieve with our aftercare program is to really go through the Wheel of Life, discover what you want to do, and get you on a path to get there. We can't actually stop the criminal behavior, and we can't solve the welfare cycle of dependency unless they get gainful employment. So that is a critical part of it.

Akeem got involved in our PACT rock music program. He is a really good rapper. It won't get him a job, but it did get him a vision for his life, which we believe makes a huge difference. I think getting people to experience the skill development program and team environment is a good way to get a spark going. So, we get them excited, and that brings us to the other half of what we do in the organization – our experiential programs. For example, our PACT fashion program participants were on the runway last Sunday, and our program was featured in *Fashion Week* two or three weeks ago. So, what I'm getting at is these are kids who couldn't put a needle in a sewing machine and now, two years later, they want to be fashion designers. That's how you get people excited.

Fran: David, I am so inspired by what you're doing. Through vision and possibility you are helping to light that flame of hope that needs to be kindled. Kids seeing other kids that have made it to places beyond what they could ever imagine – it is absolutely thrilling!

David: These types of environments get these people excited. It isn't like we have come up with some perfect formula. We have taken the time to understand how people change in a positive way, and we look at the simple principles of those environments. Then we build them. We just know that if you put some sunlight on the plant and give it some water, it's going to grow, right? And if the soil is pretty good, it is going to grow even better. But I don't have to figure out osmosis –

the universe does that. I think happiness is like that, and I think environments are like that.

Kate Sharpe

Interviewed by Fran Fisher, August 8, 2012.

Kate Sharpe, M.Ed., Certified Professional Coach

As a Certified Professional Coach, Kate Sharpe focuses her coaching on Leadership and Performance coaching. Kate's energy and expertise as an award-winning educator, researcher, and educational programming consultant all contribute to her approach to coaching. Kate is Head Coach and program co-designer for the PACT LifePlan Coaching Program.

www.katesharpe.com

Fran: Hello Kate, I understand you developed the LifePlan Coaching Program at PACT.

Kate: Yes, I was hired at the very beginning to help PACT create the coaching program. They called it a coaching program, but it actually was a mentoring program, with a strong social work component to it. Coming on board, I wanted it to be a true coaching program so that the coaching model would serve as the foundation to all that we did.

So I explained to PACT that I was going to be pretty strict about the coaching piece and I was going to incorporate the ICF Core Competencies [*bit.ly/1bDvSDW*] to serve as the basis of the work. That's where I started with the volunteers who stepped up.

I had done my own academic background research on what it takes to change health-related behaviors in youth, and that's the work I had been doing professionally for many years. I brought these two worlds together because I needed coaching to support me in the work that I was doing with the youth. I worked in the school system. I wrote curriculum for the schools in the Ontario Ministry of Education. I was very involved at the provincial national level, but never truly satisfied with what we were completely up to; I needed more skill. That's why I got certified as a coach. So I brought all of that to PACT, even though I didn't have a whole lot of experience with at-risk youth. I taught inner-city elementary school for 12 years, so I certainly knew the profile and recognized the behaviors, but I certainly wasn't an expert on at-risk youth.

I thought if they wanted to call this a coaching program, and if I'm going to have my name on it, then it needs to be a coaching program. There has to be a certain skill level and we all have to be operating in the same way with the youth for that element of consistency, especially if we were going to measure our impact. I had already been working with Craig Trowhill in the school system. I had invited him to join me working in classrooms around bullying programs, and he of course had an amazing impact. I thought if there is anyone that should be a coach in the PACT program, it should be Craig.

Over the course of five years I brought coaches on board. It started with Craig. We told his mother, Adria Trowhill, and she started to spread the word at Adler Learning in Toronto, where she was affiliated. We had a lot of people come that wanted to do the work, and so it just grew from there. Through that process I worked very closely with David Lockett, the founder. He and I had a lot of conversations around where we are at, what we want, and how we are doing – visionary type stuff. So that's really been a critical part.

I spent my first two years hammering home the coaching at all of our coaching meetings. Once a month I was doing skill drills. I was teaching foundational skills and I introduced the ICF Core Competencies. Craig helped me with that.

Sometimes he would present a teaching piece. As you know better than I do, Craig hated paperwork and hated structure, so it was always a total riot trying to teach with him. But, just having him in the room was gigantic, and that's what was so hard for me over the course of my relationship with him. When he went through some very challenging times prior to his death and he wasn't there a lot, I missed him so much. I missed his presence and his clarity around what worked and what didn't work and what coaches needed to do to connect with kids.

Fran: Yeah, because when he was physically there, he was fully present, wasn't he?

Kate: Well, I would say a percentage of the time he was distracted like we all are. I knew his full story, though. He and I spent a lot of time talking about his life and all that he had experienced, and so I was able to cover for him when he didn't show up sometimes. I'm sure just like you did, you had to go, "That's Craig!" Maybe you gave him shit next time you talked to him, but he always had a valid reason why he wasn't able to be there. To me it was a real testament to his honesty and his authenticity. If he wasn't capable of being there, he wouldn't come and fake it. Craig didn't fake anything. If someone were to come and ask me, "What is the critical piece in the PACT coaching program?" I would say it was the dynamic with Craig. I brought the formal structure and he brought the spiritual.

Fran: Kind of balancing of the being and the doing.

Kate: Right. The structure and the process, so where the two circles intersect is where the magic happens. Sometimes we get too far one way or too far the other. Part of any challenge with work like this is that it can slide around, or you get someone that's operating on the fringes, which happened where we had to let go of some coaches because they were advising. I'm not saying there isn't a mentoring component to the PACT program. There are times where the coach needs to teach them to go get health care, how to take them to the eye doctor and buy them a pair of glasses, or find them a bed to put into their apartment. You know the mentoring pieces around basic life skills, but I can say that everyone that is coaching in the program now is really committed to building capacity. And that was always my thing with them. If we really want to do what we want to do here, we have to build capacity in these kids so they can stand on their own two feet outside of the context that they have become so connected to – the at-risk behavior and the unhealthy relationships they were involved in. So that in a nutshell was my role. Most important for me was to support the coaches in the line of work because it's a game of inches: two steps forward, three steps back most times, and if it was easy, more people would be doing it.

> We have to build capacity in these kids so they can stand on their own two feet outside of the context that they have become so connected to – the at-risk behavior and the unhealthy relationships they were involved in.

Fran: Where do you see the LifePlan Coaching Program today as you are transitioning out of your role at PACT? And what is needed going forward?

Kate: Today it's truly a coaching program grounded in the coaching skills and the measurement tools we use to gauge the difference we're making. We have modified a variety of different coaching-based tools to use them as measuring tools for our work, which is critical if we want more funding. We are privately funded. Not a penny from the government, which always amazes people. We are also at a critical juncture where the groundwork has been laid. In a perfect world, what would happen next is it would be more formalized. There would be a manager who was properly paid to run the program, who would also be a lead coach that would help coaches with their coaching skills, the kind of skills you need to coach youth.

Fran: What is needed?

Kate: It's having a stronger infrastructure in place. I would have binders for the clients and a handbook for coaches and have all of the structures to support continuity. We have those now with measurement tools that we use as pre and post assessments with the youth. It's starting to emerge. It's a very organic process. It's a real juggle between enough infrastructures to support the process, and driving the process. The process takes over and people get so bogged down in the process it burns them up and they quit. It's finding that fine balance and being able to work with people who are experts at supporting at-risk youth entering into the community, which is our primary purpose. Also, we need strong leaders that are committed to the spirit of the work, because there are lots of people that want to do the work.

Fran: One of the pieces of Craig's vision for this book was that it would attract more funding so that more coaches could actually get paid.

Kate: Yeah, for someone like Craig, it could actually be a full time job. So, where do we get the funding?

Fran: What if you had the funding you need?

Kate: David is talking about moving it into the school system in a much more purposeful way, because we are getting a lot of these kids when they're 17 or 18, which is tough. They are pretty hardwired at that point for somebody like us, so we are trying to move back a little bit and get them further upstream. So, how do we get referrals from the school system, or from the teachers? As a teacher I could have told you immediately which kids would have benefited from working with a coach. You know who you're going to lose. The school system isn't going to pay for it, but it would be increasing the reach.

Fran: What is something important to you, a message you want to share?

Kate: Wow, well I was thinking about that driving here today. The title, *The Illusion of Hopelessness*, was really ringing in my ears and I was thinking that's exactly it, because it is an illusion. I don't even know if it's so much the youth's illusion as it is the system's illusion. What I truly believe about people is that everybody has the capacity to change within them – everybody, no matter what the circumstances. So, within the confines of a strong relationship – a connection with another individual – that can really be the launching pad for transformation. The coaching skills and all of that are obviously important, but at the end of the day it's the quality of that relationship. That's the size of the portal you've got to move back and forth between. I just want everyone to know in the whole wide world that we want to help kids who are in the system. As it is now, they are just in the system and they just roll around until they are coughed out the other side.

There is an opportunity to change, but it requires a relationship and a structure – a coaching and a capacity-building process to support them in the work. It's not about fixing them; it's not about rescuing them. It's about strengthening capacity.

> It's about strengthening capacity.

Now sometimes I say, "Yeah, Kate, that's great. You've got to wake up and get out of your bed of roses," because there are a lot of other circumstances – and I get that. There is the socioeconomic situation. There are, nine times out of ten, addiction issues, so there is all of that, which needs to be a part of the equation. But I think if we all operated like we do as coaches, what's important is what's right, not what's wrong. The traction is going to be in that domain. That's when change is going to start to happen. It doesn't have to be complicated. That's one of David's great messages: "Let's keep this super simple." I think he is spot on because it is easy for it to get complicated.

Fran: I agree, and that brings our conversation full circle, actually, because that is the secret of Craig's success, and Shawn, who I interviewed earlier today. They share the same ability to meet these kids where they are with authenticity, and it's that simple – maybe not easy, but a simple formula for success.

Kate: Craig and other people in the system have told me this: "If you have been on the street and you have been a part of a gang, the kids look at you differently." So, no matter what, at the end of the day I still didn't walk the walk with them and Craig did. He would understand the silence. He would understand the anger. He would understand the absence. You know, it's like a peer coaching program. How do we bring youth back into our program as coaches? Shawn, one of our new coaches, is kind of on a leading edge. He hasn't been through our program yet, but we also have youth that have graduated from the program that have come back to meet with other youths. It's the capacity-building part. If you are telling people what to do, you are preaching. They are going to become dependent on your preaching, and that's what happens to so many of the programs that I see. People become so attached to the person and the person delivering the guidance, their own abilities start to retract. We need to be weaving ourselves out of the equation.

Fran: What other challenges do the coaches have in working with this population?

Kate: Some of our coaches had trouble building rapport, which is something you can teach someone to do. If a coach can't gauge when it is happening, it's a challenge for them in working successfully with their clients. We had one coach that wasn't very open to the idea. This was a challenge for her to do. Craig coached her masterfully. He was so honoring of her. He helped her see the opportunity to create an impact as a coach, and then she was totally open to the idea. He really worked from the inside out and helped her find "it" within.

Fran: What's the client side of that equation?

Kate: Being in a place where they are ready to be coached. They may not know it, and it may take them awhile to understand what the relationship is about because it's very foreign to them. They are so used to people telling them what's wrong with them, and what they need to change.

Fran: Changing the subject just a bit, education raises their awareness of options they didn't know were available, doesn't it?

Kate: Right, absolutely, and I have been thinking of clients that we have had in the program regarding the idea of attending a university and taking them and showing them the university, walking around talking about programs in the university. We actually have one of the youth who came from a very challenging situation and he has just applied to architecture – a direct result of the awareness-building exercises. It's been transformational – and this is an immigrant family whose son saw nothing but his court charges sitting in front of him. And for every one of those, there have been lots of youth that we haven't been able to reach.

Fran: What's one of your favorite Craig stories that isn't one that is really well-known?

> We have to hold a big space for these kids.

Kate: Well, I have lots of Craig stories. Craig taught me a lot. I guess the one that really stands out to me is what he would say over and over again: "We have to hold a big space for these kids." He would use a wide variety of metaphors to explain what he meant. For example: *If you hold a small space, they will be small; if you hold a big space, they will be big. You have to be patient* *because they are inside their houses. The door is locked, the blinds are pulled, the bars are across the door, and they are inside, and you are on the outside. You have to be able to sit on the outside of that door until they are ready to at least take the bar off and maybe peek at you underneath the window shade.* Craig would just talk about how he could see that happening with the youth and eventually the youth would come out because trust is like a speck of dust in this building. It is so hard to find in them because their trust has been so violated so many times in so many horrific ways that learning to trust a total stranger is the foundational piece. So it was "hold a big space," and he would laugh seeing me here with a pen and paper and file holder. "What is all that bullshit?" he used to say to me. "What are we doing, just tell me what we're doing." And I would say, "Craig, I brought you an agenda. I'm helping you here." He would always say, "The universe is always on my shoulder." And I would just have to trust him.

I told a story at Craig's memorial service. It was when one of his former clients came to a coaches' meeting. Craig said he was going to bring a client that had just graduated from the program. So this youth came. Craig and the youth sat at the front of the room and the coaches asked questions, and that's when I asked this youth, "How would you describe the coaching process that you have been involved in with Craig?" It had been over two years because this kid had reoffended and it was challenging. He said to all of us, "You know, when you're living a life of crime you're moving in a very fast-moving river. It is very fast and very dangerous. You have to be watching all the time. If you let your guard down, something is going to happen. What so many people try to do in helping us and fixing the problem is they try to extend their arms and help pull us out of the river." He said, "What Craig did was jump into the river with me and he talked to me as we went down the river together, and he talked me over to the side."

One time Craig had a kid on the run. The kid would bolt from the courts. Craig was on the phone with him. He said, "You have a choice. I'm not going to tell you what to do. So let's think of your choices. Don't tell me where you are because I'm going to have to tell people where you are." And the youth talked to me about that and reminded me how you always have choices. And that is capacity-building; that is increasing awareness. That youth wanted to go on and be a youth and child worker. I've got to tell you this guy was arrested with an AK-47 machine gun – like this guy was a really serious dude. And now he wants to be a child and youth worker.

Fran: Oh, that's fantastic! Those stories are so inspiring – gold nuggets for others who want to make a difference.

Kate: Yeah, this is something I found after the memorial service. It's all about trust. Craig wrote it:

Trust. One of the most important factors in dealing with any client, especially young offenders, is trust. They come from all walks of life, yet share similar life experiences. It could be abuse from a parent or trusted person in their lives. It could be from being around other violent, angry, scared kids if they were or have ever been in custody or jail. It could be from being in a gang where trust is given very sparingly and even then... Often they come right from custody, jail, or a courtroom, at least. They are told where to stand, what to say, hands behind back, empty your pockets, etc. etc. They do not trust others. They are suspicious and scared. Despite their crimes, they are scared young people, and often children. The key thing is to get to know and support them, without prying or being overly pushy. They are like wounded wolves with no pack. Trust is hard to come by and it takes longer to rebuild it once it is broken.

Fran: What you said at the memorial service, do you have that written?

Kate: Yes, I have a copy right here.

Memorial service, July 11, 2011

Craig's impact was all about his masterful ability to access a direct line to the hearts and minds of the kids and young adults everywhere we went.

Now, make *no* mistake. Craig was a serious rascal. He did not play by anyone's rules but his own. He had to be reined in at times, in a coach-like way of course... his Mohawk dialed back, his fresco of tattoos appropriately veiled or his colorful language adjusted. His serious allergy to paperwork or reporting of *any* kind also had to be managed.

Periodically small doses could be ingested, but on the whole, any type of "paper" – as he called it – was ignored or neatly folded up and put in his pocket... and politely returned... never used.

He used to tease me endlessly about my stellar lesson plans and timing instructions in our sessions together... he'd never *ever* pay *any* attention to any of it... and I always knew, as many of you know who worked with Craig... that my job was to get us organized, set the stage, give him the Coles Notes version of the program, buy him a coffee, and then let him go.

With the finely tuned sense of a cougar, and with an intense integrity, patience, profound wisdom earned from a complicated life, and with a direct line to the "universe"... he'd roll up his sleeves and begin.

My memory of Craig is just this: His ability to create a safe and trusted space for all of us whilst courageously holding an unwavering commitment to "possibility and hope."

As he said many, many times in our work together with PACT, where he served as Assistant Head Coach, our job is to "offer the perspective of hope, possibility, and forgiveness without judgment" – in his words, "Our job is to hold a big space, for our clients to live into it."

That's what I learned from Craig. It's plain and it's simple and it's damn hard to do well.

The stylin' sage, the warrior, the rascal, my friend and collaborator, Craig. Thank you, Craig. You have left us all with a job to do. Kate

Will Manos

Interview by Fran Fisher July 10, 2012.

Will Manos is an Adler International Certified Coach and is currently contracted by PACT Urban Peace program of Toronto and The John Howard Society of Belleville, Ontario, Canada (*www.johnhowardbelleville.com*) – both award-winning organizations. Will specializes in empowering and supporting at-risk youth to fulfill their life plans. In the last several years he has worked all over Ontario with many high-risk youth offenders and supports these youths in their own environments. For the past several years Will was the lead Life Coach for a federally funded program working with 25 high-risk youths. This project has recently received extremely positive reviews from youth justice partners. Will is a certified member of the International Coach Federation of Toronto.

Will Manos, B.A., Toronto, Canada
willmanos333@gmail.com
(416) 873-6337

Fran: Hi Will! Please tell me about your work with PACT and the youth in the juvenile court system here in the Toronto area.

Will: Some of these youth have had issues with the juvenile justice system. They may choose to do the coaching and be moving forward toward their goals, and then they may choose to party one weekend, doing some drinking, and have a slip up. They may choose to be subject to a breach of something and might have to spend some time back in jail, or custody. I will go and visit them, which will give me a chance to build a relationship with them. A lot of the parents won't come and visit them and so it's a chance to build a support connection with them, but it's also a chance for reflection. Reflection can be a great opportunity to Coach them through the situation. They may have made some progress and then they f'd up; it happens.

In creating change there is often a setback, but especially with these kinds of kids; they have had so far to come in their change process. I find that it's kind of an ongoing characteristic when they do fall back that we support them while they are in the fallback. I find there are three F's they turn away in... frustration, failure, and f-ups!! I view it as a great opportunity. I can ask them, "Yeah, what did that look like? How did that work for you? What was going on for you there?" They get a chance to share in the learning of the setback. Looking in the mirror is hard for all of us.

Fran: How is that working with the court system?

Will: I don't have any issues within the court system for youth. When I work in Toronto, when I work in the Belleville court system, it is a lot smaller community, so interactions with court participants and the system supports is a lot easier to connect with.

How the program got out there was that there was a very proactive Judge there who wanted to bring the PACT program to her community. She was very positive and open to new programming and had known about coaching and was intrigued by what PACT coaching was doing in Toronto. What I found is that the probation officers and the crown attorneys classified us as another piece of the social work or mentoring. It took a whole year for them to learn the concept of youth coaching. Now they have come on board because they have seen some significant changes in some of the youths.

Fran: Wonderful. It took some time, but it was the results in the end that won them over.

Will: Yes, I believe so. And right now I see myself being a coach in the streets. Yes, I have my coaching half, but I'm really the only one in the youth circle that will go into their environment and do my work in their comfort zone in a space where there is no judgment. It adds a little bit of credibility to the youth that are deferred by the court system. Coaching is a different model than their parole officers or other social workers because the youth usually have to go in and see them at their office. I frame it more like being with the youth and going to them. These youths are living kind of hour-to-hour, in a sense. Going to them takes into account the challenges the youth face and provides a space for trust and confidence to be established. Sometimes I text them the night before, "Hey I'm coming up tomorrow. We have an appointment at two." I drive all the way, and they no-show. I truly believe it's a situation where they just forget about it; they struggle to manage the situations of life with no management skills. I'm kind of worried about making it too easy for them, but on the other hand, it allows the trust and the belief in the relationship to be built, right?

Fran: So, sometimes you wonder if you're making it too easy for them, but then you…?

Will: Well, I think there is a level I can test. I do believe giving them meeting times allows them to show and prove they are doing their work, but as far as not making judgment on the client about it, you understand who they are, by just listening to them talk, that they are moment to moment – that they don't really live on a plan. A lot of these kids are couch surfing and have incredibly reactive lives.

Fran: It's a reactive lifestyle, living in the moment, isn't it?

Will: Very much.

Fran: What coaching principles are most important for you in working with these youths? And, why?

Will: I think *Establishing Trust and Rapport* would be number one, and then *Active Listening and Direct Communication*. Direct Communication means authenticity, you know? Yeah, so those are important as far as the coaching principles, but then there is that huge piece about the client – that they are capable, creative, resourceful, and whole; that they have their own unique strengths. I think they are called "anchors of self." Those really show up with the youth.

Fran: What is a specific client story that you would like to share? Where was the client when they started working with you? What were their issues?

Will: I had a client that graduated with PACT. He was honored by PACT and we have stayed in touch like in an aftercare situation, which is really important. We will hook up and we will text and meet up for a cup of coffee once a month. "Tony" had lost his father when he was really young. He had an issue at age 15 at school. I think someone had stolen his hat; he got really angry and assaulted the kid with a pencil and he got kicked out of school. And he was having other issues, as well. Tony was under house arrest when he came to PACT. He was 17 when I started working with him. I worked with him for a year and then he graduated from the program. He battles a little bit with alcohol and cocaine – struggling with the influence of friends and the street. He wanted to go back to school to get his GED, but he got a job instead. He really enjoyed cooking and he got a job at a restaurant and built up his skill set and confidence at some of the restaurant's franchises. Tony is pretty active and he has been holding down a job in the restaurant industry. He has moved out on his own, established himself in his own apartment – and he just turned 19. I got him involved in a leadership camp with Rotary Club. He applied and got accepted and actually leaves this Sunday.

Fran: That's wonderful. What a great success story!

Will: It's been a two year process, though; he lost his job about three weeks ago on some sort of sexual harassment. He was at a party with a female co-worker and she claimed some stuff and there were some issues that happened and he ended up losing his job. So he texted me and we met and talked about the lesson there. We both have a restaurant background so we connected about partying and people you socialize with from work. There is a learning and a growth and life lesson in that, but it was in the reflection that he could understand. He is really excited about this leadership camp and that he got a new job this last week.

Fran: I'm curious, in terms of your personal experience as a coach working with these youth, what are your personal challenges?

Will: I think I have always been able to see individuals as *capable, creative, resourceful, and whole* because I have a tendency to want to lead. I keep coming back to "it's not my work," as it is really their work. I'm getting good at it, but as always, it is a process. It is emotionally draining work and the process is very up and down. As I always reflect, you can't give what you don't have. I'm pretty strong on the clients being capable and letting go so they can figure it out at their own pace. It takes patience and having trust and relying on that, as well as being in the coaching position in the moment and dancing in that moment without being fearful of regression or failure. Am I making sense?

Fran: Absolutely, it makes sense. It's emotionally draining and it takes patience. So how do you keep that reservoir within you? How do you keep it full?

Will: I really just trust in the coaching process and my belief that it is the client's work.

Fran: That's strong trust and an empowering belief for you, as well as for your clients.

Will: Yes, I trust the process and believe in it – dancing in the moment is kind of how I envision it too, so it's comfortable with me. I know the process is happening and that I need to just be in the moment and show up for the youth, whether it's an anger outburst, a sensitive issue, or just being where I am supposed to be at an arranged time and letting them cancel the appointment and fail on themselves.

I had another issue with another youth, "Merrill." He loved rapping and loved writing music, so that is what he wanted to do. We had a conversation about the fact that getting high all day wouldn't support the fact that he is going to need a job to support his music career. Eight months into focusing on his writing and rapping, Merrill was offered an opportunity to perform at an event with the John Howard Society of Belleville. The John Howard Society is a nonprofit agency in partnership with PACT. They are an organization committed to fairness and dignity for high-risk youth.

Fran: Oh, terrific!

Will: Yeah, so he ended up performing in front of people for the first time. Leading up to that event though, we had a coaching session right before he was going to a rehearsal. On our way over, he had to stop in to see his probation officer. The PO gave him a hard time for not doing his stuff, and Merrill got angry, and said, "F**k this rapping and PACT stuff!" He was really pissed off, you know? So I stayed with him in the moment and let him say his stuff to his PO, and then we went back to the car and we had a coaching session and reflected about what just happened. I kind of felt sorry for the kid because he was under a lot of pressure. He was being a bit dramatic with himself, but just staying in the coaching, holding the focus on what he really wanted, and reflecting on all the work he had done, he ended up understanding, and we ended up proceeding to his practice session. He felt so good after his performance. He felt so fulfilled! So I brought him back to that moment where he could have thrown it all away. Yeah, framing that understanding, and acknowledging the courage it took him to let his anger fall off of him, and not act on his aggression, and not self-sabotage himself, right? So I acknowledged that in him... acknowledgement is a very key tool in this youth coaching method... it could be on the littlest thing, but it's a great tool.

Fran: How wonderful that you could be there with him in the moment, anchor that win for him, validate him, and help him see how heroic he was being for himself! How would you describe your coaching approach, Will?

Will: Sometimes I am a coach, sometimes advocate, sometimes cheerleader, supporter... I envision a copilot supporting my clients in their plane of life. Whether it's going to their appointments or whatever. We

> I envision a copilot supporting my clients in their plane of life.

have conversations on bad drivers, courteous drivers, etc., framing life challenges and their reactions and consequences. When I am a copilot with them, my point of view is that those are opportunities that I get to connect with them, and that's part of our work together. So, sometimes I coach, and sometimes I copilot. It's all about opening up the opportunity for the coaching – meeting them right where they are.

Fran: Got it! And that's a key to your success.

Will: Yes, and with the high-risk youth specifically.

Fran: Back to the challenge in working with high-risk youth. You said, "I have this tendency to want to direct, and I have to manage that, and sometimes it's emotionally draining, and it takes patience." How do you take care of yourself so that you have the strength in the moment to self-manage?

Will: I think it is about listening to myself. I make tapes of mentors or use literature to kind of anchor myself back in the process, and then through each challenge there comes opportunity to apply what I am learning.

Fran: That's the kind of thing I'm curious about.

Will: We have a coaches' meeting monthly. I'm pretty self-reliant, but we do have an opportunity to share our stories at our PACT meetings every month; I think that's important too. We can collaborate and draw on other peoples' stories, like a coaching community of support. I draw from my own personal life experience too.

Fran: It's important for you to leverage from your own strengths and experience, isn't it?

Will: I find it supports me.

Fran: What has changed in your personal life working with these high-risk youths as a coach?

Will: It has helped me become a better coach. When I see their graduation and they write about the meaning that the PACT program had in their life or the support that they received – that makes it all worthwhile. So, it enhances my personal growth and my well-being. I'm a big spiritual person and a lot of my coaching revolves around karma and the universe – you know, *what you put in you get out.* So working with these youth deepens my own learning, and I'm learning how to manage my own emotions.

Fran: Are you saying that you are improving your ability to manage your emotions?

Will: Yes, and one thing about these youth is that they are very street savvy and streetwise. They really know if you are being authentic and if you're really there with them. It's funny because a lot of them will ask me early on, "Are you getting paid for this?" They want to know if it's my job. For the first couple years I did it voluntarily for PACT. So in terms of the ICF Core Competency, Coaching Presence, the kids are very in tune to why you are here. I want to be part of something that is more than a service, like handing a beer over the bar to someone to self-medicate. That's why I do this, to give them life-enriching tools, rather than in my previous career when I sold beer to them. I was in service, but I wasn't in service congruent with my values.

Fran: So this service is meaningful for you and it's making a difference. Congratulations! You are connecting your life and your work in a way that is fulfilling for you.

Will: That's right.

Shawn Harding

Interviewed by Fran Fisher August 8, 2012.

Shawn Harding is an active soldier for change. He believes that with the help of many people and organizations we can create urban peace.

Shawn is a LifePlan Coach & Program Ambassador for the PACT Urban Peace Program, dedicated to helping at-risk youth and building peace and hope in our urban communities in partnership with the courts and schools. Shawn founded the Shades of Gray program in January 2012. This is an initiative to work within the juvenile court system to assist youth currently involved in the system. We also create bridges to other programs to better serve the clients.

shawn.harding5@gmail.com

Fran: Hello Shawn. I would love to hear: What are you learning from working with PACT, and what is the contribution you want to make?

Shawn: The contribution that I want to make for PACT is to take what I know from the streets and apply it to working with the youth, so they don't end up in jail or prison. I've been out on the streets. I know what it looks like. I have been inside prison. I know what that looks like. So yeah, I am just trying to give back so I can try to prevent kids from going down the wrong path that I went down. I am learning so much with PACT. Growing up, I didn't have many mentors. The mentors that I had were all criminally involved; even my father, mother, brother, and sisters were all involved in different kinds of crime, and so to have this opportunity to learn about the life coaching and to connect with youth that I feel are in the next generation of me, that's just what I want to do.

Fran: That is beautiful. What led you to choose "not crime" when everyone around you was involved in crime?

Shawn: It took a lot of time with me being inside of prison. I did two and a half years. It took a lot of looking around me. I'm 24 years old, almost 25, and I have been to 42 funerals. I have watched all my siblings pass away. I watched people get addicted to drugs. I watched what's happening in the news. I watched all the sadness that I have seen over the years, you know? I watched it every day.

For me, crime is an easier way. I can make a phone call right now and get back into my old lifestyle, but that's not challenging enough. Causing systemic change is challenging, so that we don't have to go through the jail system, so that people that live in these priority neighborhoods have full representation, and they can have a better lifestyle. It's easy to say what made you choose this and what made you choose that. Lucky for me I got out. A lot of these youths are living this lifestyle every day. They're not looking at tomorrow; they're looking at survival right now.

What we have to do is build programs that are sustainable, like hiring youths for jobs. See, I don't see a major gang problem in Toronto. I mean if you have a certain address, you're not going to get hired, no matter what you do. It's a hiring problem. Instead of putting money back into police and bigger jails, they need to put money into jobs for the youths – job creation. What they're doing now is boring. It's been going on forever.

Fran: Shawn, I am hearing that "challenge" is a core value of yours.

Shawn: Yes, it is. I mean when I was 15-16 years old I was making three quarters of a million dollars [CAD] per year selling cocaine. To me that wasn't challenging enough. That was easy and it cost me everything. It cost me time that I won't get back. It cost me family. It cost me the creation of my own family. It cost me a lot. I never finished high school. I only have three credits from Grade 9, so going to a university was not in the picture for me for a long time. I had to hustle to get into a university. I had to find back ways to get an education. I had to live out here in the shelters and streets. So yeah, it's just not challenging enough to sell drugs. It's not hard. That's all I was, an importer-exporter. So now I just want to meet the clients and see where they're at, because I understand where they're at. I understand that they can't take time out of their day to talk to me if there is no bread on the shelf.

Fran: So it cost you quality of life and you are building that back for yourself. Now you have a job.

Shawn: I work six days a week, plus everything else. I am serious about my schoolwork. I take seriously what I do inside the community because I work full time at an auto shop, but I also work as a community support worker in priority neighborhoods. So right now I'm working in all 15 priority neighborhoods in Toronto. When you're on the streets there is a system. Why not overcome that system and bring it back to where it's supposed to be?

Fran: So you see that there is hope?

Shawn: Of course, there is always hope. If there were no hope I wouldn't be here. That's what keeps me going. I know what I have to do. I know what I'm doing. The joy that I get from

> There is always hope. If there were no hope I wouldn't be here.

seeing kids come off the street and get success – I have no hate on them. What we need to start doing is give back in our own communities. Instead of community organizations going into the communities we need to empower the communities.

Fran: So that the people in the communities are building their own capacity.

Shawn: Exactly. All these other organizations want to do flash-in-the-pan programs and they get paid a lot of money for doing a consulting thing, and then six months later, when there is no more funding, they fall out and do something else, and people in the priority neighborhood know this and that's why they don't attend the program. They feel these organizations are jokes. If you want youth to come to your program you have to realize youths are out in the street making money. Their view is: "Why are we going to give up money to come to a free program, when we need that money to survive? If you pay us, we're there. We don't want to sell drugs. We don't want to shoot each other. No one is happy, but we're not going to give up our only means of survival for nothing." That's the reason why the drug game is so popular. You don't have to have a resume.

Fran: And those skills are transferable. I mean, you're running a business, right?

Shawn: Of course. It's all about money. It's all about making a profit. It's all about shipping and handling and customer service. It's all there. The only thing is because it is an illegal business the risk is higher. The benefit is higher, but also the punishment is also greater, so if you have Burger King and McDonald's on the same street, Burger King can't go over and blast McDonald's. They have to come up with their own marketing strategies. But because it's an unauthorized business we don't have to play by those rules, so we do what we do.

Fran: How long have you been working with PACT?

Shawn: I have been involved with PACT since last August. Last August I contacted PACT about volunteering. They told me about life coaching. I'm doing my practicum at Adler Learning International next and that starts in November. I have just been working with PACT kind of on the sidelines, just giving advice where it's needed, being that person that bounces ideas – giving PACT ideas on where they should be heading next. I see a bigger vision. I am a big picture person coming from the streets. I had 50 employees underneath me. I started doing this when I was seven years old. So, yeah, I am a big picture person. I like to see a lot of things happen. I don't like small change. I like big change.

Fran: Let's talk about coaching a little bit. What are you learning about coaching that is meaningful to you?

Shawn: For me, what's meaningful about coaching is the conversations that we have. I talk with youths regularly on things that are meaningful for them. They call me up at three o'clock in the morning, or dinnertime, or whatever, and we have conversations. So for me it's applying these coaching skills to conversation. I really enjoy conversing with people.

Fran: Are these empowering conversations? Are they conversations for accountability?

Shawn: Yes, when PACT started talking to me about coaching with young offenders I thought, "Cool, why not?" That's my family. That's my extended family. So to me having these conversations, it's about seeing where they are. It's not about bringing them to a fancy office. I'm comfortable walking down the streets with them.

Fran: And that's what coaching is supposed to do, but I do a different kind of coaching. I'm on the phone with people that can afford to pay me. They have lives and businesses that they want to improve, but I'm also getting right alongside them the same as you are. It's the same in that I'm listening to them right where they are.

Shawn: Again, for me this concept of coaching really is amazing because for once I'm actually going to be able to do what I have always wanted to do, and that's about talking with these youths about what's going on in their world. It's about going through the whole program and giving them a whole different outlook when I talk about mentorship. I'm talking about role modeling, meeting them where they are, and understanding where they're coming from. A lot of people from the streets can't afford education, so where we got our education is watching other people do things, which is mentorship – one of the oldest forms of education. It goes back from African tribes. You sat back, observed, and you learned from your elders. I believe any behavior that you learn you can also unlearn. I deal with that on my own. I'm very hotheaded. I get frustrated fast just because of my lifestyle.

> I believe any behavior that you learn you can also unlearn.

It's just different when you live in a violent world. To survive, you have to be more violent than everybody else. So you have to learn how to be more aggressive. Now I have to sit back and try to reverse that and cope with that.

Fran: In coaching we call that self-management.

Shawn: Exactly, and that's for me one of the biggest challenges coming from that lifestyle.

Fran: What you're learning is how to use your authentic power.

Shawn: Not enough people care, and for me my goal within coaching is to care about these youths. They talk about kids being in gangs at 14 or 15. We have to start talking about youth that are in gangs at age 10. We need to start focusing on this demographic before they even reach 14 or 16. They won't always hear you, but with coaching I love the way it's set up inside that conversation, because that's all I'm doing. I'm not advising. I'm not saying you're in the wrong. I'm not saying, "Listen, you really messed this up." I'm not judging; they already know this.

Like I said, everything that's been happening inside this city is boring to me every year. It's the same thing. We're having the same talks. They invite me down to the police headquarters for the same chats every year. They invite all my friends to all have these discussions. We told them what we think, and every year they tell us we don't know what we're talking about. When they get funding, they're not going to run a youth program. They are going to hire more cops. Right now we have so many inmates that are waiting to get into prison. They're talking about building a 10,000 inmate jail, and when they're done building jails they're going to fill them.

Fran: What about the youth coming out of jail?

Shawn: When you're working with people that are getting out of jail it's always a different thing. It's a whole different thing. Coming out of jail is a scary thing. When you get your release date you are thinking, "All right, what am I going to do with myself? How am I going to survive so I'm not back here?" And all your parole officer is saying to you is, "You have to get a job."

Fran: Hey, Shawn, you did it! Congratulations! You did it. You didn't go back to jail.

Shawn: It took a lot of dedication. A lot of people won't sit here and work for minimum wage. You know I'm 25 years old and I make [CAD] $10.50 an hour just living day to day, but I know where I am headed.

Fran: PACT is grateful you are on the team.

Shawn: Me too.

Fran: And these people see who you are. Look how you are being supported. The PACT team recognizes your wisdom. You are an important member of this team. I look forward to celebrating the contributions you make in the next few years.

Jude Delsoin

Interviewed by Fran Fisher July 11, 2012.

Jude M. Delsoin is a Certified Practitioner in Synergology and an Adler Trained Coach. She assists individuals to reconnect with their unique strengths, values, and authenticity to achieve a vision. Jude has a unique talent and passion to inspire people to feel good about who they are. She is also a writer, empowerment performer, a public speaker, and workshop creator. She provides coaching services to visionaries, leaders, and writers who search for clarity, confidence, and strength.

www.jmdcoachingservices.com
info@jmdcoachingservices.com

Fran: Hello, Jude. What is a core belief that guides your approach to coaching?

Jude: I am guided by the core belief that we are all unique, resourceful, and whole. The coaching approach leads to more confidence, clarity, and strength. When I know what my strengths and values are, it's easier to make decisions, and to move forward with a personalized plan. This is how I see it.

Fran: I can see how our philosophy helps you be effective when working with your PACT clients. You are calling for your client's confidence, strength, and clarity, and helping them learn their value.

Jude: Yes.

Fran: What is important to you about your work with PACT?

Jude: What's important to me is that I am glad to be a part of a group who believes in urban peace. It doesn't matter from which background the teenager is coming from and what's happened in their life, PACT respects the youth, and that's what I love. The organization always tries to see which of its program would be more beneficial to the youth: the LifePlan Coaching Program and/or one of our many life and job skills based projects such as PACTFashion or PACTCooking. It's important for a youth to learn different types of skills in general so they can find work, go back to school, and develop coping strategies to be able to take their place in society. It's amazing the change PACT is creating, and that is why I continue to coach with them.

Fran: So, you are proud to be a part of this program.

Jude: Yes, I am very proud to be a part of this program. People will ask me, "What do you do?" and I'll say, "I coach youth through the PACT organization." Sometimes I'll send interested people to the PACT website to learn more and I also invite certified coaches to attend one of our monthly coach meetings so that they can explore the opportunity of becoming a PACT Life Coach themselves.

It's very fulfilling because when I was doing the Adler's Coach Certification program people asked me, "What do you want to do when you finish the program?" I said that I want to work with at-risk youth. Someone asked, "Are you a social worker?" And I said, "No, while I believe that the coaching tools that I've learned can be used with adults from all walks of life, why not also use them to support at-risk youth as well? Some youth do not have positive caring role models or the strong presence of their parents in their life and can end up in very challenging situations because of this. Why not use the coaching skills as a stepping stone?"

I think everybody has a role le to play in the community. Everybody can have a positive impact in someone else's life, and that's why I am so passionate about working with youth at risk.

So it's actually fulfilling for me to contribute to the life of a young person because I believe young people are the future. If they can impact their family, they can impact their neighborhood, their community. They can impact their city and maybe eventually their country – we don't know. That's why it's really important for me to use the coaching skills and apply them to working with young people.

Fran: I congratulate you for finding a place to fulfill this desire to make that kind of contribution. You found a sweet spot where who you want to be is what is needed in the community.

Jude: Thank you. I have always had a desire to impact youth.

Fran: What kinds of results do you achieve with your PACT clients by taking the coaching approach?

Jude: Well, first of all, I align with what the client wants. The types of results that I see are building self-responsibility, and for them to know who they are and to always be aware of who they are being; how to be their best and how to apply their best to go where they want to go in life – and that they can apply it now. So, I can say it is a discovery of themselves – raising their self-awareness and then being able to make some choices and to act on those choices, because they know what they have inside of them they can use this to go for what they want. Most of the time the wealth is inside of them, not outside of them, and most of the time they're not in the proper environment as other types of kids. That's why they have to find strength inside of them to go for what they want.

Fran: Yes, it's a powerful support structure to have a committed relationship with a coach, as well as knowing that the whole PACT environment and organization has got their back too.

Jude: Yes, they do have a community of support, but I believe what is most important is PACT is not giving them a fish. PACT is giving them a way to fish. That is what is really powerful.

Fran: It's helping them to find the strengths within to build capacity for themselves. That builds their self-esteem and self-confidence, right?

Jude: Yes, and for sure it takes time to create that, especially with youth. Coaching a youth is different than coaching an adult. It takes more time. In the beginning, when I am asking questions I will receive a lot of "I don't knows" and "I never thought about it." We get a lot of that kind of reaction. It takes a lot of patience and the need to create trust.

Fran: You have been given the gift of patience or you wouldn't have been able to stay in the work. What is a success story you can tell me about a youth you helped in their self-discovery process, accessing their strength and then taking it forward?

Jude: Okay. When I saw "Billy" for the first time he looked really stressed. His facial expression was really tight. He was smoking a lot. The first time we met he mentioned he had an interest in acting. I scheduled weekly meetings with him and he was pretty consistent. He would show up most of the time. If he was unable to come he would call. This was a youth who had no interests in school. He had dropped out. He didn't like it. He has a brother and they were both reporting to a probation officer. He had a friend that wasn't a very good influence on him and he was smoking a lot of cigarettes to cope with his stress. He was living with his father and he would go see his mother during the weekends. Every time we met, I would focus on asking him questions about his passions and his visions and what's well in his life, and how to create more out of what's well. He was passionate about martial arts and this is how he also connected with Craig over time. There was a time when Billy was arrested by the police, but from what I understand, he wasn't guilty. He didn't really do anything wrong, but I remember Craig being very supportive. Craig called me because Billy's dad could not find him. Craig went out to look for him and eventually found him after many hours. I really feel like Craig went way beyond the call of duty in supporting me and in helping my client, who was obviously going through a very challenging period.

When "Billy" came back to the coaching sessions after being in detention, he was a different kid. When his father called me to tell me he was worried, in my heart I wasn't worried because I knew that the kid I coached was a different type of kid. He knew that he needed to have self-control in life, not to fight all the time, and not to be rude, especially with police.

He had learned through the coaching that he needed to be respectful at all times because being respectful impacts his freedom. So when he came back we continued the coaching and we continued to talk about his passion and what he wants out of life.

He was so positively impacted by the coaching it started to impact people around him, so some of the other youths around him changed. This is what he told me. He told me that he started to coach his brother and his brother wanted a coach, too. His father said, "Okay, if you want a coach then you better call Jude because she is a really good one." So I ended up coaching both of them at the same time, and this is something PACT doesn't typically do. We usually do one-on-one, but this time I coached both brothers. They were so close in age they were like twins.

It turned out to be beneficial for them to participate in the coaching together so they would keep one another accountable. They learned that they are different. Before the coaching they thought they were the same. After the coaching they were each able to find their own path. When you don't see yourself as unique you confuse yourself with someone else and then it can be a problem to make choices.

So knowing that they are both individuals, but they are also a team, was some of the awareness that they got from the coaching support. Neither of them like school, but through the coaching they decided they wanted to go back to school because they had a vision of the future – something bigger. The school didn't want to take them because they had previously had lots of problems with school.

Fran: I have a good feeling about how this is going to turn out.

Jude: Through the coaching they learned that each action has an impact. They became more determined on what they wanted. I coached them about that. What they did was really impressive. As I said, the school didn't want to take them. No one was returning the calls, so they went to a school in another city that was willing to take them.

It took them an hour and a half to go to school. This is how determined they were, because they had a vision of a positive future. Now they knew why they had to go to school, because of what they wanted in life. So they went to school and they also participated in the PACTRocks music program.

They quit smoking. Through our coaching conversations they realized that smoking was blocking their progress. They identified the difference between when they smoked from when they didn't smoke, and how this affected their martial arts training.

At the end of the coaching they were only smoking one cigarette a day, and then later they sent a report that they both had stopped smoking completely. So, yes they got into a new school, quit smoking, and they also cleaned up their environment. They were no longer hanging out with those friends who had been bad influences. Going forward they were more careful of who they chose as friends.

After the coaching they continued to take responsibility in creating their future. They had learned how to talk to people, and how to ask for what they want, and how to research for what they want. I received an email from one of them after the coaching and it said, "Jude, I was an extra in a music video." For me it's a gift to see a kid who will embrace the LifePlan Coaching Program, and be responsible, and continue to use their strengths and talents in their life.

Fran: Well, that's your fulfillment, isn't it? It goes beyond satisfaction. You created an environment for their success. You helped them access their strengths and values, and use them as self-empowering tools for creating a new future. They got it so clearly from their experience that every action, every choice they make has a positive impact. I like what you said: "they had something bigger." What has changed in your personal growth in the time you have worked with PACT?

Jude: There is something I have learned working with PACT based on experiencing the difference in working with my first youth and the second youth. I learned to focus on the vision and all the joy that we will have when we accomplish something. I have learned that focusing on the pain doesn't serve us as well as focusing on the gain. Focusing on the pain can help motivate someone into action, but it might be tricky because that might attract more pain. After that experience, I help my PACT clients focus on the potential for gain not pain.

My first way of coaching was to help get them out of trouble. Now my coaching is not like that. The coaching is about something much bigger than the trouble. And that's something really important. That is something I can apply to myself. I was listening to this CD the other day about this man who had success from happiness. Did you see the movie *The Pursuit of Happyness*?

Fran: Yes, I did. It was based on a true story. Very inspiring.

Jude: Okay. I was listening to a recorded interview of this man sharing a story of his life, and he was looking for happiness. He was trying to get out of poverty. He was trying to get out of pain. He just wanted happiness, and then he became a really successful man. I have been experimenting with that with my coaching. That's why in my coaching and in my life I focus on positivity.

Fran: You are a strong woman, Jude. I'm curious, back to these two brothers – what a great success story, by the way. As you were working with them through their process, what were the challenges for you as a coach in working with them?

Jude: The challenges at the beginning were that they wouldn't do things. They would stay home and sleep. They didn't have any motivation. Their main challenge was their addiction to smoking because smoking is what actually drained them. But the challenge for me was that they didn't feel motivated to do things, like go to school. The challenge was about personal problems at home.

But I didn't focus about that during the coaching. I focused on other things. Coaching for them was a fun space, but their life was difficult. The stress that they had as young people was an obstacle.

Fran: What was challenging for you personally as a coach while working with them?

Jude: I can say that working with them was a perfect match. That's why at that time I never saw anything as a big obstacle. I always see it as a space of growth and I would ask them at the end of the session, "Okay, what is the situation, what have you learned about yourself? What can you do next time that's different?" This is how I was going around their obstacles. But what was really hard was going around their procrastination, but I held it as an area for growth. Now that I think about it, the main challenge working with these youth is that they didn't like to talk. The biggest challenge, though, was their environment, their friends, and the fact that they didn't have healthy role models in their lives.

Fran: So when they didn't want to talk, or when they were in that procrastination mode, I'm wondering, what did it take from you to deal with those challenges?

Jude: Sometimes I used what I call empowerment poetry. I would read a poem and then ask questions about the poem. Sometimes I used storytelling. I would tell them a story and then I would ask them questions about what they learned from the story.

In coaching my clients, there are activities that are creative, too. It depends on the youth. I will invite some of them to write something or draw something. If not, then a real challenge is a youth that comes from a neighborhood where there is not much hope. I would ask, "What do you want to do after high school?" And they would say, "I never thought about it. I never thought about doing anything because my parents never did anything, and my grandparents never did anything." They don't see the need for having a vision.

Fran: How do you turn on the light of hope or vision?

Jude: In coaching it is about sharing a light of support. It's about supporting the light and then growing the light. If the person does not have any fire, it's about assisting them in creating that fire. If they are willing to create that light,

81

anything is possible. So how do you turn on the light in a youth that doesn't want to create? That is a real challenge.

Fran: It is important for us as coaches to acknowledge we only play a part. We are not the "be all" in their journey. We are a stepping stone. We have to trust that is enough.

Wendy Fortune

Interviewed by Fran Fisher August 10, 2012.

Following a graduate degree from the Johns Hopkins Carey Business School and a rewarding career in Human Resource Management Consulting, Wendy expanded her expertise to include coaching. Although she works with a variety of clients in her Career and Life Coaching practice, it is her specialized work with youth who are in conflict with the law that has proven to be the most rewarding. Believing in them, respecting them, and supporting them empowers and inspires these young people to turn their lives around.

Wendy Fortune, MA, ACPC, PCC
Birkman Certified Consultant
www.fortunelifemanagement.com
(416) 953-8120

Fran: You earned your coaching credential with Adler Learning International in Toronto, and your Associate Certified Coach (ACC) accreditation with the International Coach Federation, is that right?

Wendy: Yes. I also have a BA in Psychology and Political Science, and I have a Master's in business.

Fran: My goodness, you have been a lifelong student! Congratulations. You bring all of that experience and your heart to PACT. They are blessed to have you on the team.

Wendy: Thanks, it has been very rewarding for me.

Fran: Wendy, what's important to you about your work with PACT?

Wendy: It's about making a difference in the lives of young people who are really struggling with figuring out who they want to be. That's the way I see it. It's a very different kind of coaching experience, and they are just trying to find themselves. It can be very confusing for them, particularly in light of whatever experiences they have had before they get to the program.

Fran: I understand you have one client that you have been working with for a year and another one you have met with twice, so far. What positive results are you beginning to see with the client you have been working with this last year?

Wendy: Well, I'm really just helping him to figure out what he wants, his values and strengths, and what's important to him. These are things that he has never thought about and he certainly hasn't thought of his accomplishments. He has been very focused on his failures. So I think that has been big for him. Also having him trust me has been huge. It took a long time. "Danny" has had a very hard time up until now. As a young child he would trust people to love him and look after him, but they often let him down and abused him. So his ability to trust is very low, and also his confidence in people who really genuinely care. He still struggles with that. I think he trusts me now and I think he knows that I am there no matter what. There have been indications that he knows he can count on me. That is a big step for him.

Fran: That is a big step and it says a lot about who you are being, that you see and feel and observe this increase in him feeling safe with you to give you that trust. What did that take for you to accomplish?

Wendy: It has taken a lot of patience, and really interestingly, something that comes up from me all the time is his agenda. What I want to communicate to him in terms of coaching is really secondary to developing his trust and intimacy. We can't move forward with the coaching unless we have that. So that is what I have learned.

Fran: Hence the patience. You know you want to help him move forward. Nothing is going to change until you have a level of trust and rapport that has Danny feeling safe enough and ready to make changes. Meanwhile, it means you have to have enough patience and a level of sensitivity to honor where he is.

Wendy: Yeah, and here is something else I am learning: Acknowledging another person comes very easily to me. I think it has been difficult for Danny to receive my acknowledgments, because he hasn't been acknowledged enough in the past. It has been hard for him to receive my acknowledgements, but I think he gets that I'm genuine about it. When I tell him something positive that I am seeing in him, I'm really being sincere. I think that is helping his self-esteem. It's better than it was, but it still has a ways to go.

Fran: How wonderful and rewarding for you to see this strength growing in Danny.

Wendy: What I've also discovered in this relationship is there are things that are going on in his life, so he is experiencing highs and lows, and when we can celebrate those highs together it's wonderful. Sometimes we take a step back when he is having a low time because something happened that he is having difficulty with. That actually just happened recently. He has had a lot of change this past year. He has attended two different schools and started at one foster home and he is now in another foster home, but at least he has been in the same one for a while. He had a lot of resistance to this current foster home. It has been very difficult for him. Recently he lost his year. He didn't make his year. One of his top values is love of learning, which is really interesting. Not that I have a lot of experience with PACT clients, but I've been told that is a pretty rare number one value. I think that the disappointment for him was pretty high.

Fran: Let's back up for a second. What did you mean when you said "he lost his year?"

Wendy: He didn't pass. He had to repeat his school year, and retake his courses again. He is a bright guy. I haven't tested him or anything, but I know he is a bright guy. He grasps things quickly and it's his value for learning that keeps him curious and so he knows a lot. He is a perfectionist. When he moved schools and had too many assignments, he felt overwhelmed and then got behind. I later found out that he just wouldn't do them if he didn't think he could do them 100%. You know it's difficult, but I have confidence in him that he can get his act together and really move forward. But he has to be able to believe that too.

Fran: What were Danny's key issues when you started working with him?

Wendy: His number one issue was he wants to be loved and he doesn't feel loved or cared for. His father was abusive and his mother didn't want him. Finally he stepped up to the plate and said I'm not going to take this abuse anymore and that's how he ended up in foster care. I think he had hopes that his mother would be there for him, but he knows that she just abandoned him. So that is what he is seeking in terms of his life right now.

Fran: You have already mentioned it takes patience. My question is: What are your challenges with working with this client?

Wendy: Well, certainly, continuing to be patient. Building trust and meeting him where he is – and just letting go of my agenda. Allowing him to set the agenda and go where he needs to go. I realized it was very difficult to build the trust and I committed to myself that I would spend as much time as required in order to do that. So sometimes that has been a struggle. I know he has the potential to move forward. He has to trust me and he really has to trust himself. I have to step back and allow him the time that it is going to take to feel safe and to feel like he can trust me. It may take a lifetime until he completely trusts himself. But he is on the right path.

Fran: What are or have been some of his obstacles?

Wendy: I would say certainly not trusting adults, low self-esteem, believing that he is not worthy of anyone caring for him. He can be very stubborn and opinionated. He has had some huge assumptions and some beliefs that tend to get in his way. And there is safety for him in holding onto those assumptions and beliefs. I recognize that. So those are certainly obstacles for him on an ongoing basis.

Fran: Has he developed any new empowering habits or beliefs that you have observed?

Wendy: I would say that Danny is just now ready to start establishing some new habits. I wouldn't say that he has been ready up until now. He paid lip service in wanting to do certain things like establish goals, but I think he had a lot of different issues that he had to sort out and deal with first. The fact that he is still staying in the foster home that he is in now is important. There was discussion with the Children's Aid that they were going to move him to another foster home. I originally thought that might have been a good thing, but as it turns out, they are going to leave him where he is. I think that is the best thing. He needs that stability right now. I think that even though they might not be demonstrating in ways that he appreciates, they do care for him. I think that they are giving him the boundaries, and that in itself for a teenager is a way of showing that you care. He has trouble with that, but I think that is something all teens go through.

Fran: How old is Danny?

Wendy: He is 16.

Fran: Is there anything else about coaching Danny that stands out for you?

Wendy: Yes. In terms of Danny's assumptions, some of them have been challenged. I have challenged those assumptions, so he is thinking about them. He is starting to trust me, which is huge. He is learning what his values and strengths are and that is something he didn't know before. I often go back to those and think that it is huge for him to have that knowledge. He has survived a very traumatic year of change. He is staying with this foster family. He definitely wanted to leave for a while, so I think that staying there is a really good sign. I mean, he had input and he didn't always have the final choice, but I think he saw when he discussed it with me that staying would be the safer move. He doesn't know what he would get if he moved with another family. At least with this family he knows what to expect. It may not be perfect, but nothing is perfect and I think he recognizes that. So that has been a big step.

He is learning how to deal with what life throws at him; not everything is perfect and all of us continue to face challenges in various areas of our lives. He is starting to establish better coping mechanisms.

In terms of habits, I could say at one time part of the reason that he was in trouble with the law was his anger. He is learning to manage his anger better. When he does lose it, he recognizes it very quickly and is quite regretful and will apologize, and that's progress. So I guess you could say that anger is a habit he is changing.

Fran: Do you have any expectations about the coaching process in working with Danny that are not being met?

Wendy: I do. One of my unmet expectations is regarding the Wheel of Life and other coaching tools. Danny has not moved forward with some of his goals on his Wheel of Life, or if he has, he has stepped back as he got closer to the school year, because he had stuff that had to do with academic goals, and that was all the bench strength he had at the time. I think going forward, having the stability of staying where he is living will help him to be able to focus more easily on his other life goals. And, he does have a support system outside of the foster parents, me included. He also sees a therapist, so he does have a support system that is pretty good that will hopefully help him move forward. Also, now he will have a tutor come to his home and work with him on assignments. One of the big goals of course is to have him graduate high school so that he has options for where he wants to go from there. He originally told me he wants to be a CA [Chartered Accountant]. Danny also has an extremely passionate interest in astronomy. He could tell you so much about it. So he had hopes of getting involved with NASA. So he has some pretty high goals, which I think are wonderful and I have encouraged him to pursue.

Fran: What are some tools that you have used to help him overcome his issues?

Wendy: I used the Wheel of Life. I used future visioning, and the Learner/Judger Model by Marilee Goldberg (http://inquiryinstitute.com). He loves to read magazines while we are talking. I used to struggle with that a bit because I didn't think I had his full attention, but I finally realized that was a comfortable way for him to carry on with our conversation. One time he landed on a picture of John Travolta. He was just gazing at the picture. At first he made it clear that the picture really related to him, so I asked him to tell me what he thought John Travolta was thinking. He went into quite a bit of detail on what he thought John Travolta was thinking, and he said, "That's really me." He was basically saying he was letting go of the past. He was gazing out into this very bright future. I used the VIA of Strengths, a value clarification exercise, and I often use attunements. When he sees the pipe cleaners in my briefcase he says, "Oh no, not the pipe cleaners!"

Fran: Are the pipe cleaners an attunement? What are attunements?

Wendy: Yes, the pipe cleaners are an attunement I use to begin engaging the client at the beginning of a coaching session. I invite the client to take a pipe cleaner – any color that they like – and I ask them to shape it into something that represents where they are "at" in that moment. Danny doesn't really like the pipe cleaner exercise, but some of my other clients love it. I ask them to draw where they are coming from on one side of the paper and where they are now on the other side. Then I ask, "What feels so much better about where you are now?" Or, another attunement I have offered Danny is to just pick a word that represents where he is in the moment. Or, I ask him what his level of focus is or his level of energy in the moment or where he would like it to be. In terms of coaching competencies, I have used a lot of Direct Communication, Active Listening, and Powerful Questioning. Danny complains to me, "You ask way too many questions," but he also understands that's what I do.

Fran: Say more about how Danny has responded to those activities.

Wendy: Sometimes he responds really positively, and other times not so much, so we just move on. What I have found is there are acknowledgments that really seemed to have helped. He hasn't had enough people in his life that have recognized him for what he does well, so that has been really powerful. I'm also remembering a time when he was allowed to move back to his old school. He met with me right after he found out he was going back to that school and he was so elated because he had friends there he was comfortable with. Sharing in his highs and celebrating with him was very positive and rewarding.

I also used one tool that I often offer. He tells me he would never use it, but in his head he knows what it is. With a guy like him, where he does have a temper, people can push his buttons and trigger that anger. This is a very useful tool. It's called the STOP tool. I just love it. You Step back, Think, Organize your thoughts, and then Proceed. I have mentioned it to him many times and he says, "No, no, I'm not that type of guy," but he understands the tool. I hope he will integrate it into his life at some point. Maybe the fact that he is losing his temper less often, when he does lose it, he is immediately recognizing his mistake.

Fran: My belief is that we do plant those seeds and they do nurture in ways that we may never see visibly. We can trust they have some influence. Wendy, I am so inspired for who you are being with this client – your creativity and your commitment to making a difference. What have you learned about yourself in this PACT experience so far?

Wendy: I've learned so much! The biggest thing has been learning about meeting the clients where they are. It's so true, because I want to help them move forward. On my own time, I think about various tools that might help, or conversations we could have that could excite or encourage them to share with me. But what really matters is to allow them to set their agenda, go where they need to go, and if it's possible to introduce various tools that are going to enhance that experience, then great! But really just letting them have control – that is huge.

Fran: What growth or learning has allowed you to be more effective or more successful at meeting the client where they are?

Wendy: Just letting go of what I think I am supposed to be accomplishing or doing and just letting it happen. Not orchestrating it in any shape or form – that has been huge.

Fran: I'm sensing the idea of *trust*.

Wendy: Well, certainly trusting myself with that whole idea that the client, even with all their problems and being so young, they are creative, resourceful, and capable. They will find their way. I don't have to parent them. I just have to be there, trusting the process.

Fran: What differences in your own life have you noticed, as a result of what you have gained out of this experience?

Wendy: There is no question that my life is fuller. I feel a kind of reward coming my way that is just from being in the relationship. It goes back to the whole thing about wanting to make a difference in someone's life. It's doing it on such an intimate level because I am

> I'm not focusing on their failures or what they feel are their failures. I'm seeing the best in them.

showing that person that I care about them and that I respect them and I see the best in them. I'm not focusing on their failures or what they feel are their failures. I'm seeing the best in them. For me to see the best in them, help them realize that they really have some great qualities, and they can make a difference themselves – that is enriching my life.

Justice June A. Maresca

Interviewed by Fran Fisher October 25, 2012.

The Honorable. June A. Maresca

Justice: Ontario Court of Justice

Central West Region-Peel Regional Municipality-Criminal Court
100-7755 Hurontario St.
Brampton, Ontario L6W 4T6

Fran: Hello, Judge Maresca. In your courtroom you worked with Craig Trowhill and his clients from the PACT LifePlan Coaching Program. What did you appreciate about Craig's relationship with those kids?

Maresca: What impacted me about Craig was the way he connected with everybody, not just with his clients. Yes, he was there, he showed up, and he listened, but he had lived a lot himself, so he had credibility.

The first time I met Craig was for a Section 19 conference. This is a meeting where I can invite anybody involved with an offender: the parents, parole officer, school board member, anyone associated with the youth's particular interests, and, in this case, PACT – to attend a meeting to develop a plan for a young person to help ensure he didn't reoffend. Craig was there. The kid did not show up.

Craig was completely cool about it. He said, "No problem. Whenever he is here, we will be back." This is an important point. In some segments of our society, there is an expectation that once a kid is charged, that's the end of it. But, that's not how it works. They are still kids. Their brains are not able to see the consequences of their actions. They fall down again. What we need to do with these kids is follow through on the consequence imposed and then show them how to move on. It's a teenager's job to test boundaries. When kids make poor choices, parents don't disown them. They say, "Here are the consequences, and here's how we move forward."

> They are still kids. Their brains are not able to see the consequences of their actions.

Craig didn't give up on kids. The PACT Program doesn't give up on kids.

Here is another example about Craig. This was another Section 19 conference. We came up with a plan for the young person, a good sentence that addressed his needs and would help to ensure he wouldn't reoffend. I think Craig felt I was being too soft on the young man, so he said to him, "You better not screw this up! This is a good deal here."

Craig would be there again and again and again. And this was consistent with the PACT Program. At home, if the kids had a home, they often experienced lots of rejection. Kids in the PACT LifePlan Program got to learn how to own their self-worth and experience another human being who cares.

Fran: What would you say is critical for success in preventing recidivism?

Maresca: Gaining trust is, of course, critical. Another critical piece is taking small steps to learn to be personally accountable. And, what's huge is when they can come back and report that they are doing well. Once I sentenced a kid to 18 months' probation. He was big kid with little affect, and when he spoke, he was monosyllabic. I asked him to come back in two months and tell me how well he was doing. He came back in two months and he looked different. He was more animated. He reported doing better at school, his grades were improving, and he told me that he had received an award from an organization that seldom gives out awards. He brought the award to show me. I said, "You must be so proud of yourself!" And then I told him he didn't have to come back before the 18 months was up, unless he wanted to. He said, "Yes, please." He came back a couple of months later to show me his report card.

Fran: What would you say are the key success factors with the PACT Program?

Maresca: One of the key success factors is that they work in conjunction with the court system. Many of the kids seem to respond well to having the presence of someone of authority on their team.

What was important about Craig, as a life coach, was that he was personally turning himself around and giving it forward.

The three key factors that will keep kids from re-offending:

1. They are accountable.
2. They are achieving something and doing well.
3. They are developing empathy.

What prevents recidivism is when kids can look at people as people who have hopes and dreams versus seeing people as things. This is what impresses me about the PACT Program. For example, in their cooking program, the food they prepare goes to feeding the homeless. In their fashion design program, the kids make prom dresses for kids who can't afford one to wear to a school prom. In their urban farm program, the fruits and vegetables go to the local food bank. Their kids are learning how to pay it forward. They develop empathy when they know they are helping others.

> What prevents recidivism is when kids can look at people as people who have hopes and dreams versus seeing people as things.

Justice Richard Blouin

Testimonial Letter from Justice Richard Blouin, Ontario Court of Justice, Ontario, Canada

January 9, 2012

To Whom It May Concern,

Re: PACT Life Plan Coaching Program

About ten years ago, when I was the manager of youth prosecution in a busy suburban Toronto youth court (Scarborough), it became clear to me that not enough was available to assist seriously involved youth. Often young men were sentenced to substantial periods of time in jail, but when they were released they had no lasting positive direction and little assistance staying on track.

The Life Plan Coaching Program was developed by PACT in response to my concern that these young men, who were ready to turn their lives around upon release from jail, did not have the skills or guidance that would allow success. Since these were the most difficult kids who were committing a disproportionate number of serious offences, and would likely continue to do so for many years, the financial and societal costs were enormous. Also, since these were the most difficult kids, I felt that turning their direction away from crime and toward a productive life would yield at best a success rate of one-in-ten. Even so modest a return would yield significant returns.

However, in the eight years the LPC program has been operating, the success ratio has been much higher. My own experience in referring kids, and those of other judges I know that have referred to LPC, has been overwhelming. In my view, LPC is the best chance to prevent a 15 or 16-year-old in serious trouble with the law from becoming the 35-year-old with a seven-page criminal record.

As Kevin O'Leary's new CBC show, Redemption, Inc., will illustrate, if you don't assist these young men now, society will pay exorbitantly in the future.

I am happy to speak to anyone about this program.

Sincerely,

Justice Richard Blouin

Ontario Court of Justice

Section Four:
Coaching Youth at Risk

Jason Wittman

Interviewed by Fran Fisher November, 19, 2012.

Jason Wittman, MPS has had a private practice as a life coach since the middle 1980s. He received both his B.S. degree in Business Management and his Master of Professional Studies in Counseling Psychology from Cornell University in Ithaca, New York. He is also a Certified Hypnotherapist and a Certified Practitioner of Neuro-Linguistic Programming. Jason specializes in coaching parents of adolescents and young adults.

http://MyCoachJason.com
http://TheParentsCoach.com

(818) 980-2929

Fran: Hi Jason! What is your background with coaching? And please tell me about the way you work with youths and their parents.

Jason: My background started by figuring out that what I was doing – that I was calling counseling – was basically teaching people life skills and then coaching them through those skills as they learned how to utilize them. In 1983 I actually had a name for what I was doing. I called it "Life Coaching."

Fran: You were a man ahead of the times!

Jason: Actually I had parallel careers. I started a therapeutic community for drug addicts in 1971 while I was still in grad school at Cornell. That led me to starting my first street program. A lot of the flavor of that was captured in my novel called *The Street Shrink Chronicles*. I didn't know what I was doing. Most of my courses at Cornell were counseling and psychology mixed with social work. They didn't teach me much about street work, so I decided to sit on the same wall where the street kids hung out in a permissive part of that town where all the college kids lived, and make it up as I went along. I wanted to start a youth program, so I went and sat on the wall. I didn't say anything to anybody, just hung out and observed the comings and goings, and especially the power structure, until a week or so later when one of the ringleaders of these kids said, "How come you are sitting on our wall so much?"

"I am starting a youth program."

"What do you do?"

"I assist people to get a job."

"So, can you get me a job?"

Of course, I had a couple in my pocket, because I knew all the merchants. So when he got his job, I was IN.

Fran: You established credibility!

Jason: That's how it started. I approached the kids the way I'd approach a dog I didn't know. I know that sounds strange. I'd just wait until the kid reached a level of comfortability. My counseling approach was very much influenced by William Glasser and his work called Reality Therapy.

This is the best book coaches need to read: *Choice Theory*, by William Glasser (http://wglasserbooks.com/books.html). It's really good, especially working with couples.

Also my whole method of operating has been and always will be at my client's level of comfortability. Later, I worked with street kids in LA. The hotline, which I answer 24/7 is all that is left of it due to lack of funding. For almost 15 years I was on Santa Monica Boulevard working street hustlers every night for 12 hours.

Fran: Those were long nights.

Jason: Yes, but I'm a night person and when you are on the street you have a lot of adrenaline. I moved about 25 kids a year off the street. A lot of times I was out there alone – my van and me, with a table in front of it. I had condoms, Starbucks muffins, and a bulletin board. If you go to http://www.la-youth.org you will see a picture of me hugging a kid, and the table and the van.

So, anyway, even there I still had that basic principle, that they have to come to you. If I saw a kid looking at the food and then looking at me, about all I would do was stop what I was doing, smile, and simply say, "It's free, you can have some," and go back to what I was doing. Responding that way acknowledges that I care, and allows them to participate at their level of comfort. My principle has always been that if you do it any other way, there comes a point where you are going to have to point out in one form or another that what they are doing isn't working. And at that point, if they have been roped in and feel like they weren't there on their own, then their answer is, "Who asked you?" And they are right. Who asked me?

So that's my first level - that it's all about working at the kids' level of comfortability.

Fran: Your approach fits with the standard coach training, which recognizes the critical importance of establishing safety and rapport first – creating a safe environment.

Jason: Agreed. On the street there is no safety – period. But there is in conversation. After the first six months my reputation had gotten to a point that I would meet kids for the first time and they were talking like they had known me forever, because they actually did know about me through the other kids. And, they assumed that I knew everything.

Fran: Say a little more about that lack of safety on the street.

Jason: If you are in a street situation, gangs would occasionally swoop in and try to rob the hustlers. No honor among thieves, but there could be safety in knowing that whatever they tell me isn't going to go anywhere.

Fran: And you really made a point of that in your book – how you were absolutely steel-trapped in that regard.

Jason: Yep! I once won a showdown with the County District Attorney who threatened me with jail if I didn't divulge information about my kids. I showed up at his office with my toothbrush and paste and said I was ready to go. He backed down. I learned another lesson in that area. I once told the older brother of one of my kids, who was concerned because he thought he was involved in some store heist that his brother wasn't involved in. And boy did I hear from that kid. He said, "You don't tell my brother anything! Even if it's good." So, I learned that lesson. And I applied that to family members too. Every once in a while I coach kids and their parents and I tell them both that I might suggest things that are absolutely contrary to what I've told the other person, because I am just going to work you through your stuff and totally forget about knowing anything about the other side.

Fran: And that's what we call confidentiality in coaching.

Jason: Incidentally, because of the way this all evolved for me, I personally do not see very much distinction between coaching, counseling, and, for that matter, the kind of therapy I used to do. I really use them all synonymously.

Fran: What else would you say are principles that are key to your success in helping kids build capacity and move themselves out of risk?

Jason: The very important thing about building capacity is this: There is no way to build capacity without teaching basic life skills. They are not going to learn life skills by asking them curious questions. They are not going to get it that way. That's why I particularly like Dave Buck's approach at Coachville, because Dave's an old soccer coach and his whole principle is you can't coach the game until they've learned the game. With kids, they don't know the game yet.

> There is no way to build capacity without teaching basic life skills.

Fran: What do you have to say about "hopelessness" or lack of motivation?

Jason: You still have to start there before they are even open to learning skills. Learning skills doesn't mean how you brush your teeth. The number one skill kids need to learn is to like themselves. This is probably the biggest principle I learned in grad school. It was a course on counseling kids. One of my professors told us that in working with kids, we have the wrong take on underachievers. He said underachievers are typically treated as a motivation problem. They are brilliant, bright people who are dropouts and getting lousy grades, and hanging out with the wrong people. It's not a motivation problem. It's a case of very smart people who are highly motivated to not succeed. They are intentionally trying to fit in with everybody. They are thinking and acting like losers and when that happens, they voluntarily take themselves out of the competition. That's a key understanding in working with kids.

> The number one skill kids need to learn is to like themselves.

The symptoms of that are all the symptoms of not working up to one's potential, stage fright, and all the different addictions. The bottom line in working with kids is teaching self-confidence and self-esteem stuff, and coaching them through that is probably the most fruitful thing any teen coach can do. You might as well hear my favorite exercise...

From now on, anytime you see your reflection in a mirror or storefront, you must do two things:

1. Smile
2. Say one nice thing about yourself.

Even if you don't feel the smile, you must fake it. One nice thing means a verifiably nice thing – not something that you really don't totally believe is true about you. If you use the mirror to beat yourself up, you need to say two nice things for every nasty one.

I get more opposition about doing that, but eventually when they do it, it's actually the thing that changes their life.

Why the smile? When you smile you can't be down and smile at the same time. When you smile you change your state. And if you do this regularly your face becomes a trigger to a smile. So eventually it will be an automatic process.

Fran: That's cool. It's simple, doable, and repeatable. What do you say that enrolls them in taking this on and getting their promise to do it?

Jason: With youths I talk to on the crisis line, I might not get to talk to them ever again, so after we deal with their presenting issue, I'll throw this in, and they'll remember it, but they might not do it for six years. For kids that I am working with regularly, this will come up as a remedy when there's a window of opportunity.

Fran: What else would you like us to know about your work with youth?

Jason: There is a parents' section on my website www.theparentscoach.com. You will find access to a book by William Pollack, Ph.D., called *Real Boys Workbook*. Pollack is the director of The Center for Men at McLean Hospital, a major teaching facility of Harvard Medical School. The Center is dedicated to enhancing knowledge of men's life experiences and physical and mental health issues. He is the expert on how to reach and counsel boys. This workbook is the "how-to" version of his original, monumental book, *Real Boys: Rescuing Our Sons from the Myths of Boyhood.* This is a must-read for anyone interested in working with boys. He has teenagers down pat. I saw him interviewed on the Oprah show three weeks before the Columbine event, and he was talking about the boy-code (http://www.williampollack.com).

The boy-code is all about how men, from the womb, are taught that the only emotions they can show are funny or happy ones. So to ask a teenage boy, "What's wrong?" you are only going to get a grunt, and that's about it. According to Dr. Pollack, the way to get to a teenage boy about his feelings is to hang out with him for an extended amount of time – at least three hours, preferably someplace boring, like fishing – no cell phone – no car radio – and then be silent until they have enough confidence to start to talk. That's when you ask only curious questions or ones that will help bring out their feelings – not taking charge of the conversation – letting them go, and hopefully, eventually crying, if it's really sorrowful things. That's the only way to get to boys' feelings. He made this statement on Oprah that I will never forget: "When boys can't cry, bullets become their tears."

> "When boys can't cry, bullets become their tears."
>
> William Pollack, Ph.D

Morgan Rich

Interviewed by Fran Fisher, September 25, 2012.

When Morgan Rich, MA, PCC, is not coaching, mentoring, or speaking to parent or teen groups, he is laughing, playing, reading books, and enjoying every day while raising his two young children with his wife. The combination of his coaching and parenting is the most important and joyful work he has ever done. These experiences and a Master's degree from Northwestern University have helped him understand that at the heart of our success as people is a strong sense of self and connection. It is with the passion to make a difference in people's lives, and his coach training at Academy for Coach Training (now inviteCHANGE, www.invitechange.com), that he coaches his clients to sustainable and long-term success. Morgan is author of *Launch Your Life: 5 Secrets to Knowing What You Want in Your Teens, College Years, and Early Career.*

http://www.playhuge.com/my-book/
explore@playhuge.com
(503) 475-8294

Fran: Hi Morgan! What does your coaching look like in terms of working with youth?

Morgan: I have a program that I do in 12-week increments for teens and college students who are looking to launch their life, figure out what to do with themselves, or are struggling with ADHD/executive function challenges. I meet once a week over the phone and/or in person. Then I use text and email to stay in touch with them during the week. I also do coaching for an organization called SuperCamp.

I'm really good at structuring coaching calls to get clients to their appropriate level of challenge. I do this by asking what the client's agenda is, what they want to get out of the 12 weeks and also each session, and then doing really good listening. I find that I end up having conversations with teens and college students that aren't happening otherwise, but that they are really hungry to be having.

Fran: What is the age range of the youth that you work with?

Morgan: I work with kids in high school, college, or just out of college – essentially 15–24 year olds. I also work with a lot of their parents because they want to know how to support their kids. The best scenario is when I'm coaching both the kid and their parents, and then the parents are able to integrate the work we're doing. The sweet spot for me is working with an adolescent person in their transition between childhood and adulthood.

The way I look at childhood is you're at home and you're safe. You're a kid and you don't have to worry about the world so much. And then as an adult, of course, you're independent and you're out in the world. How do we get from that young dependent stage to that independent place? Well, we have to learn how to get there, and that is what adolescence is. It's really looking at how can I be safe in the world? What skills do I need, what talents do I have that are going to help me out there?

It often happens that parents think that the kids are supposed to have arrived somewhere when they are in adolescence, so they get disappointed when there is no success. I provide this perspective: In order to learn, you have to goof up. When my clients make mistakes I often say: you're doing great! This is the time where you are learning to be in the world by banging in to the world.

You can't expect them to have things perfected, like their ability to organize themselves, make good decisions, know how to plan, and such perfected if they are only 15. This is their time to learn how to navigate all this stuff.

Fran: So you are offering parents a perspective that supports their sons or daughters in making a more successful transition?

Morgan: Yes, and it's about that young person becoming a healthy human being. Many times our young people are lacking the skills that are going to help them be healthy human beings. We spend so much time and energy on making sure they know algebra, but not so much time making sure they know how to make friends, how to make decisions, and learn from mistakes.

In many cases, there is a lot of time and energy focused on grades and school and college. I'm not saying that those things are not a place where there should be attention, but I am saying that we need to put more attention on making sure our kids are happy, healthy, motivated, and prepared to step into the challenges of the world.

Fran: That makes great sense to me, Morgan! What is important to you about doing this work with youth?

Morgan: I really struggled as a kid. I never felt like I belonged. I felt like everyone else got it, but I didn't. I happen to not have been destructive, but I was all kinds of oblivious.

I heard a story this last week of a young woman who ended up almost dying because of a nervous breakdown. She had done everything she was supposed to do; she got good grades, had good SAT scores, and went to the right college. What she realized when she had her nervous breakdown was that she had lost touch with her heart. She spent so much time caring about grades that she had never paid attention to what I call the dream that lives in your heart.

It happened to me and I think that it happens to many, many young people today. I'm a very heart-centered guy and I felt massively lost in my life for a long time. I care a lot about people. I never felt the skills and abilities that I bring to the world – listening, caring, intuition, connecting to people – were valued when I was young.

I felt like I was stuck in a place where THE path was to know how to write a five-paragraph essay and be a good student. And I sucked at writing a five paragraph essays and I wasn't a good student because everything seemed so abstract (not that I knew that when I was in it).

What I know about many young people is there are abilities and passions and energy that live inside of them that aren't being valued, and so they don't come alive. The reason I do this work is because we need the creativity, passion, and courage that lives in young people in our world today. The energy and compassion in our young people is dying inside of them because they are trapped and there is no one listening to what is living inside them – whether it's a middle-class white kid or a homeless Latino kid. They have gifts to bring and I do this work because I have the ability to listen and be with them and help them discover that there is something inside of them that is real, alive, and valuable.

Fran: Because you were there yourself and you know.

Morgan: Yes, and I'm 42 and I feel like I have done a lot of hard work to find myself, and to figure out that I'm okay in the world and I'm not crazy, and there is nothing wrong with me and I'm not broken and alone. It's been a lot of hard painful work of finding this place and I will feel good if I can help someone find that place in less than 20 years like I did. I felt like no one understood who I was for a really long time – most importantly me.

My self-discovery started when my dad died when I was 18. It was a massive wake-up call for me. It catapulted me into my life. The first five years I was sad and hurting and really alone. But, his death in a crazy way also felt like the greatest gift of my life, because it woke me up. We have all heard stories about family members dying or some huge event happening and it waking people up.

My big question and curiosity is *can we please wake up without tragedy*? Tragedy happens and that's life, but the game I'm in is how to wake people up to the bigger and deeper lives you crave. I mean there has got to be difficulty and pain, those things are an essential part of self-discovery, but how we can find it ourselves instead of waiting for some crazy event to happen.

Fran: Yes, there is still work to do but you can be the wake-up call – the non-tragic wake-up call. So now you are giving back in a way that makes a difference.

Morgan: Yes I am and I am grateful to be able to do it every day.

I was assisting at this mentor camp program where I spent six days in the woods with all these amazing young men, and I was reminded of the day before my dad died. He was in the hospital and I went and took his hands and I remember saying to him, "Please take my strength because I'm strong and I have it to give and I want you to have it so that you can keep on living." I just sat there holding his hands just hoping that he would get better. He didn't. He died the next day.

Looking back on that moment, I feel like what happened in that moment was that he gave me his energy and the gift in his heart and said go live this. Go make a difference.

The tragedy of his life is that he was hidden his whole life. It turned out that he may have been gay. I don't know for sure. Whether he was or not, he never was being who he wanted to be.

His death woke me up to my desire to help people not be hidden. I realized my gift in helping people connect their dream that lives in their heart.

Now, there is no way at 18 I knew that, but I remember when I was crying and so hurting that I didn't know what to do and a phrase – "it's about people" – came into my head, and in that phrase my gift was born.

In all the tears, anger, and pain, I began to feel like I was starting a quest to discover myself. It took me a long time – why does it have to be so hard? But I got there by fighting through all of the hard times.

I guess one thing that I'm really proud of is that I didn't run from the pain and difficulty. I didn't numb it. I'm both grateful and amazed that I didn't fall into drugs or alcohol or anything like that. I don't know how I didn't do that, but I didn't. I was damn committed to figuring out what that dream was and what the gift was that I could feel deep inside me, but couldn't understand yet.

Fran: It was really a calling, and you actually answered the question that I was thinking of asking. What motivated you forward? What called you forth out of that pain, and kept you on your quest?

Morgan: It's hard to describe.

Fran: You couldn't *not* answer the call. Right?

Morgan: Yes, that's exactly right. One of my teachers said that the two hardest things you discover in your life are: one, never knowing who you are, and the other is knowing who you are. When you don't know, it sucks. You feel totally lost and confused. I spent many years wandering and searching.

> The two hardest things you discover in your life are: one, never knowing who you are, and the other is knowing who you are.

When you know it you, can't not do it. You have to do it and that can be really difficult. Once you know it, not living into it would be like cutting your arm off. I had something inside of me that I knew was there and I had to find it and do it. I couldn't *not* do it. I would have died if I hadn't done it. I felt really alone with it because no one helped me see it and I was just a kid, so I didn't understand or know how to find it or to know what was going on inside of me.

I feel like one thing we are really bad at in our culture is we get way too wrapped up in the academic success game. When that happens we just miss the human beings who are there.

I felt like I was waving my arms and screaming "Help me," and no one did. The just asked how my five paragraph essay was coming along. I feel like that's what our young people are saying today. They're screaming, "Here I am and I am hurting. I'm in this classroom and it's not making any sense to me. It's not fun or interesting, so why is everyone telling me to do better at this? I don't get why this is important - and I've never heard a compelling answer."

It's a really huge missing piece and too many people end up compromising their Self. Just look at the college dropout rates, the amount of pot smoking, binge drinking, depression and anxiety in our young people. It's alarming.

So this thing was alive inside me and it took a long time to bring words and ideas to it. I used to say to myself, "I don't know what this feeling is and I don't know how to describe it but it's clearly not good enough. If it was enough, people would be seeing me. But no one is, so obviously I need to keep trying."

But finally I realized that I am enough. It's not me that is broken. Realizing this has allowed me to give the gift I was born to give, which is helping you connect to the dreams that live in your heart.

Fran: So you changed your story "it's never enough" to "I am enough."

Morgan: That's right. I am enough.

Fran: You have made a 180-degree shift in your world view.

Morgan: Yes, it's amazing. I have said to a bunch of my friends that I feel like I just stepped out of an invisible box and now people are like, "Hey, you work with teenagers, don't you?" It's like all of a sudden people are noticing and connecting with me. It's fascinating.

Fran: And that has been a result of a shift in your consciousness, hasn't it?

Morgan: Yeah, it's really true in the work that I do with young people. That shift came out of a lot of hard work, vulnerability, and courage. We live in a culture where we expect things to be comfortable and easy. And that's okay, but I find the way to happiness and success is going right into difficulty. You've got to face it head on.

Life and learning happens in the difficulty. Parents ask me all the time, "How do our kids find themselves?" Well, they find themselves in the trouble, and the difficulty. You don't find yourself in a college classroom by reading the right textbook. You find it when someone dies, or in the grips of alcoholism, or loneliness, and the deal is that we have to be ready when those hard times come to make those choices.

> Life and learning happens in the difficulty.

You have to get good at being resilient when you get vulnerable and uncomfortable.

When we're able to stick in those hard times and go into them – not away from them. We have to be able to sit with the pain and sadness. We're not preparing our young people to stick in there very well. So I spend a lot of time with what I call building the muscles that they are going to need when things get hard.

I say "be SCRAPI, not crappy."

S - Sense of Self
C - Creativity and Courage
R - Resilience
A - Accountability
P - Perseverance
I - Intuition and Instinct

To build your sense of self takes courage and creativity, it takes resilience, accountability, and perseverance. You've got to trust your intuition and instinct.

We've got to learn how to stick into those hard places and be vulnerable because that's where you find out who and where you are. So my shift in consciousness and my being able to step into "I am enough" came on the heels of other skill and muscle building steps that got me *ready* to step into that new mindset.

Fran: Congratulations on all your hard work. It is a process isn't it? And it's step-by-step. Can you think of a story with a youth that would illustrate this process – a youth that you helped to step into the difficulty and build muscle that helped him or her find themselves?

Morgan: There was a young man I will call "James," who I started working with when he was a couple of months away from high school graduation. He was all over the place, not being able to remember homework, and just really having a hard time. So we started working together, and we started with little steps at a time – showing up. Being truthful. Doing what you say you'll do.

We talked every day from February to June to graduation. They were short calls like, "What is one thing you want to do today?" We slowly built on his successes with skills like: "Give your word/Keep your word" and "If you're not going to do it, don't say you're going to do it."

He was scared and dealing with anxiety because he was about to finish high school and head out into the world. He has a voice inside him saying, "I don't have a lot of evidence that I'm going to make it out there." There was a lot of "Whoa, this is scary!"

James and I explored ways that he could help his parents know how to support him. I worked with James's parents to build support systems for James. And I helped his parents come to understand that he was in a really important learning process, and what looked like failures were actually really important developmental steps. I helped his parents understand that he is going to fall down and he is going to do things we don't want him to do, but he is learning how to be accountable to himself.

James was making slow and steady progress. Eventually after graduation, we set up a plan for him to slowly begin to make his way out of his house. We gave him about a year where we said, "You know you're going to have to go make your way out into the world." And by working with his parents and working with him, he started to step into it.

He started to do the dishes at home. He came home when he said he would. He was honest with himself, his parents, his friends, and me. He started to search for classes at the local community college. He went and found himself a job.

He showed up for an interview one day and they said, "No, we don't have a job, but you can keep checking back, so he came back next week and a bunch of weeks after that and still no jobs. He got discouraged and didn't go for a month, but eventually he went back and they said, "Wow we're so glad you came. We lost your phone number and we have a dishwashing job. So he got the dishwashing job and within three weeks he became a line cook. He had never cooked before, but he just showed up on time, did his work, and was willing to learn.

When he got the job you could feel the confidence in him building. It was beautiful. One day, his parents were on the phone with me, crying and sharing all their amazement. Just a couple of months ago James moved out of the house, and now he has his own place and a job and he is taking college classes.

I'm just so proud of him and grateful for his scrappiness.

Fran: Good work. You stayed with him. You took the small steps to help him build his confidence and that leveraged him to independent living.

Morgan: Yes, and I really helped his parents see that all the difficulties and all the times he screwed up as part of the learning and growth process. When he didn't hand in all his homework and almost didn't graduate, it was all part of the learning and growth process, because he has to learn to show up and be accountable. When he graduated and was having a hard time, they learned to see his struggle as part of the process. They learned to keep acknowledging him so that when there was a mistake it wasn't like, "Dude, you're a complete idiot!" But instead, it was "way to make an effort and be courageous."

They began to understood and appreciate (and change their expectations) that it's the job of adolescents to struggle. They are not adults yet. They are not ready to be in the world, yet they're learning by doing, which is exactly what they're supposed to be doing. Instead of blaming them for being not enough, we have to acknowledge them for the effort, as well as hold them accountable to the consequence.

Fran: Yes they are experimenting. I remember when my son was in junior high and he was experimenting with different styles of humor, trying to find his own unique sense of humor. It was a riot. Not so fun the day he set off a cherry bomb in the school hallway and got suspended. It was so out of character for him. At the time, I knew he was experimenting, thank goodness, or I would have REALLY freaked out and overreacted.

Morgan: Yeah, you could say he was trying to find himself there.

Fran: But you are telling me that many parents don't see it like that. They see that their kid screwed up and communicate a negative judgment and that does the opposite to support them. Yes, you have a very important message for parents.

Morgan: Yes. I find it's very easy for parents to get confused and sucked into the College Acceptance Derby and expecting their kids to have it all figured out.

The way that I frame it is this: In your heart, every parent wants their kids to be good people and find meaning and fulfillment in their lives, not just get good grades.

No one wants to be yelling at their kid about doing their homework. How fun is that? Getting A's is not what is most important. You want your kid to be happy, healthy, and motivated. You want your kid to be successful in the world. Parents know that in their hearts, but it's so easy to forget it, because they are so focused on all this external stuff, and we're forgetting that life is about connection and being a good person. So, I work with the parents to try to give them their dignity back. My message is, "Here is a young person who you love who is working really hard to find their Self and find their focus in a world that is trying hard to take that from them, so let's give them love."

Fran: It's unconditional love – not judgmental love.

Morgan: In my work with parents I help them ensure their kids have a "home base". The world is hard, and each of us is in a fight for our focus and self-worth, so I encourage parents to create a place where the kids can go and not have to fight for their life like they have to do in school, class, in the lunchroom, and all over really.

Fran: One of the key principles of coaching is that we create a safe space for our clients, and Morgan, you know from your coach training that my definition of coaching is: **Coaching is the sacred space of unconditional love where learning, growth, and transformation naturally occur**. There is no fear in *that* space.

Morgan: Yes, and you can be held in your vulnerability.

Fran: Right. Someone asked me once years ago, what do you like most about your coach? I thought for a long moment, and then tears came to my eyes. I said, "What I appreciate the most about my coach is that she loves me unconditionally." Morgan, what of the guiding principles for coaching do you find are most important in working with youth?

Morgan: You have to have rapport and credibility. The establishment of the coaching relationship is so critical. You are not going to get anywhere without it, especially with teens, because they are just not interested in BS.

It's funny, you know, because I'm a middle class white guy and I've had a lot of advantages in my life, and I've been doing some work with gang kids recently. I thought it'd be hard because what do we have in common?

I was assisting at a four-day retreat in the woods with 60 kids from Los Angeles, California, and I'm like, "I'm in trouble, I can't relate to these guys." They aren't going to give me the time of day.

Well, there was a funny situation where I walked in on some of them smoking pot in the restroom, but because I don't smoke and I'm a bit naive, I didn't catch on to what was happening until after I walked out. Then I felt like an idiot as I heard them laughing.

The next time I saw them I said, "You guys must think I'm a total idiot," and I just laughed at myself with them, and asked them their names. In my vulnerability and humility I gained credibility because I was authentic and willing to re-engage with them after I looked really bad. They respected that, and that I was real with them.

It sent a message that said, "I'm solid where I am and with who I am." I realized that it didn't matter that I was a bald white guy. What mattered was that I was real and confident.

This is what young people need to know – that we are solid. They need to know that we can handle what they are going to bring because they have a lot to bring. All youth have a lot to bring. They know it intuitively right away if you are solid or not, and if you are, they're hungry for that connection.

Fran: These are the exact same words that the PACT coaches are telling me. They are working with similar kids that have been in and out of jail. You've got to be authentic – meet them right where they are without judgment, and that's a safe space for them.

Morgan: Totally. If you aren't present and grounded in who you are as a coach you are in trouble. I just don't think you are going to be able to get very far. In my work with young people they have stories to tell, and if you are a listener you could just sit there for hours and listen. I think one of the greatest gifts coaching has given me is the skill of powerful questioning. It's a skill of being able to ask the super obvious questions that seem super obvious to me, but they are really powerful. For example, being able to listen and say, "Wait, can you explain what you mean by that?" Because I think I know, and then it just opens up and opens up. I think that Setting the Foundation, Co-Creating the Relationship, and Communicating Effectively are really key in working with youth. Young kids need to be acknowledged so they know that they are being seen and heard. In terms of Action Planning, sometimes it takes a little time to get them to a place where they have the strength to be able to design actions or to follow through on action steps.

Fran: They need the strength and confidence and then they can go out and meet the world.

Morgan: And if you just throw them out into the world without the foundation, there is a missing piece to the process.

Fran: This business about being seen and heard is key in our human nature, isn't it? We critically need it as human beings. The ability to acknowledge the client for who they are being and to shine the light so they can see their own greatness, that helps clients build their core strength.

Morgan: Yes, and as a coach, you have to be able to see what they are not seeing. You have to help build the bridge for them.

I was talking to a young guy the other day. He has graduated from high school and he is really overweight. He is attending a community college, but he is sort of goofing off there and he said to me, "I am worried about making the decision on what to do next. I'm afraid if I don't make the right decision, then the next 30 years of my life are going to be ruined." I asked him, "How do you make that decision?" And he said, "I am taking a class here in electrical engineering because I kind of like tinkering around with stuff."

But then he started talking about how committed he is to losing weight, but that he would go to the mall with friends and eat fatty food because he'd forget his diet or not be able to restrain himself. He felt like he was totally blowing his commitment to lose weight.

In these two stories I heard an opening. I heard that he is being really courageous and thoughtful about taking care of himself. While not successful yet, he was doing some really hard work around his eating.

He was dancing with his difficulty of going out with friends but then forgetting he was on a diet. It occurred to me that all this hard work is where he is going to find himself. He is doing the work of self-discovery already and he doesn't even see it, because he's stuck thinking he will find it in one of the classes. "He is thinking and not feeling." To me, the gift is close to home. I think that part of the coach's role is to be able to see that and sense that and then shine a light on it.

Fran: The fact that you "heard" his courage, tells me you have the ability for deeper listening underneath the words. When you reflected your deeper listening, he probably felt more deeply seen and heard, which empowered his self-awareness. That helps the youth you serve to build greater self-esteem and confidence, doesn't it? Morgan, what changes have you experienced in your life as a result of coaching youth?

Morgan: Well I would say I'm more confident, passionate, alive, and strong. There is a strength in me and I'm celebrating because I felt like I have been struggling so hard for so long.

Fran: You are living your passion and purpose.

Morgan: Yeah, so I'm able to love more and I'm able to be loved more. I am opening to the beautiful relationships in my life and finding more friends than I've ever had.

I also protect myself more. There are relationships in my life that are dangerous, because of the judgment that comes my way. The harsh words make me fall back into questioning myself and all my self-doubt. While some of that is important, I've learned that sometimes there is a boundary that gets crossed. I've learned how to navigate that. I have gotten so much better at asking for help and finding friends and allies and professional support.

Fran: Congratulations, Morgan. I am celebrating your sense of personal fulfillment, and I am appreciating the

119

contributions you are making for a healthier world. I've never forgotten the perspective you shared with me a few years ago about youth-at-risk. "All youth," you said, "are at risk, because of the developmental stage of transition they are navigating in life."

Spark Inside

Baillie Aaron and Lola Fayemi with SparkInside were interviewed by Fran Fisher February 24, 2014.

Baillie Aaron is the founder and Executive Director of Spark Inside, a UK nonprofit coaching young people involved in the criminal justice system. She is also the founder of Venturing Out, a Massachusetts nonprofit teaching entrepreneurship to people in prison. Both ventures seek to expose latent human potential and to enable people with criminal records to achieve legitimate self-sufficiency. Baillie is a graduate of Harvard and Cambridge Universities and is a qualified life coach.

exec@sparkinside.org
www.sparkinside.org

Lola Fayemi is the Programme Manager for Spark Inside. Since qualifying as a coach with the Coaches Training Institute (CTI) in 2007, Lola has coached many senior executives and entrepreneurs in a range of sectors including fashion, recruitment, and the entertainment industry. She is now a specialist of youth coaching and committed to using coaching to bring positive change to youth justice in the UK.

programme@sparkinside.org

Fran: Hello Baillie and Lola. Baillie, we would love to hear your guiding vision and mission for Spark Inside, so we will have some context for the work you're doing, and then let's turn the conversation over to Lola who will tell us about how you're bringing a coaching approach to the work you are doing with youth.

Baillie: Thanks, Fran. We are based in London, England. Spark Inside is a fairly new organization, incorporated in 2012. We completed our pilot in 2013. I used to teach entrepreneurship in Juvenile Correctional Facilities in the United States, and what I found working with young people who have been in the criminal justice system is that there is a waste of human potential. It is the belief of Spark Inside that every young person has a spark inside of them, a driving passion and ambition to be someone or do something that doesn't involve crime.

"Success" in the criminal justice system might be measured as "not reoffending," "employed" in the education system, etc., but these outcomes may have nothing to do with a young person's goals; for example, if they're employed in a construction business, but they aspire to go back to school and study art. That does not really respect the individuality of these young people. I was fortunate to meet many young people inside of the juvenile correctional facilities who shared their dreams with me. And these were dreams of wanting to work in IT, to set up a business, to be an artist, to go back to university, to work in finance, to work in the nonprofit sector – a real range of ambitions. But one by one, what I saw was that these young people often ended up in jobs or other situations that didn't match what they wanted to do. It just seems that if a young person is interested in something, that the adults around those young people should support them into doing that. It also seems quite straightforward to me that if young people are directed toward their passions and supported in achieving them, that would be an incentive to lead them away from criminal activity.

Fran: Yes, it does to me, too.

Baillie: That's the starting place for the idea of Spark Inside. I hadn't actually heard of coaching until 2011. I wanted to design a rehabilitative program that was customized to the individual – one that took into account who the young person was, and that enabled them to explore the world outside of the boundaries either they'd imposed on themselves or that they felt were imposed on them. Those could be geographic boundaries, or they could be their own in-their-head limits learned from their environment or upbringing.

When I moved to the UK, I had the chance to explore this idea. During the exploration, it became even more important to me because one of the kids that was in my entrepreneurship class back in a Boston juvenile correctional facility was murdered. That made me think about the "what ifs". What if we can more effectively work with these young people? What if we'd had a chance to spend more time with him?

About that time I was clear I wanted to call this idea a "coaching" program. I had reconnected with my old mentor from when I was a teenager and learned that she was a life coach. So, I learned about life coaching through my mentor's experience and researching the word "coach" on the Internet.

Then I organized a group of young people who had been directly or indirectly affected by the criminal justice system. I asked them to share their experience and then to give some advice on what they would have wanted when they were in prison or what they thought their friends and family could have benefited from when they were in prison. What he or she described was this: They wanted a program that recognized the individuality of every young person – not a one-size-fits-all type of program. They did not want to be told what to do, which was interesting to me, and made sense coming from teenagers.

That's where Spark Inside got started – in 2012 when we had those initial chats. So the whole point of the organization is really simple. It is to work with 15-25-year-old youths who are involved with the criminal justice system. Why? Because the brain stops developing around the age of 25, which is probably the upper limit of Spark Inside's focus; and the lower limit is just because there are a very few young people under the age of 15 who are involved in the criminal justice system in the UK. To help these young people, who may be in prison, known to the police, involved in a gang, or on probation, we help them to identify who they are, so they build an identity that's separate from the label that has been imposed on them. In the UK they're called young offenders. In the United States they're called juvenile delinquents, or words like felon, convict, criminal, or offender. Spark Inside is about building an identity that is separate from that – a positive one that matches their values and their beliefs.

I wanted to build a program that enabled these young people to think about opportunities available to them and how to access them – a program that made them aware that they were empowered to achieve those goals. So, essentially we wanted to help move them from feeling like victims, or that they didn't have control over their outcomes, to really knowing that they had a choice. And then, ultimately what we were hoping for was twofold: first, that the young people would desist from crime, and, secondly, that they would go on to live fulfilling and productive futures contributing positively to society in whatever way they wish.

Fran: Well, Baillie, you're speaking to what is meaningful to me as well in my work as a coach. It's what I call the "inside-out approach." I applaud you for seeing that these youth were being stepped over, and designing a program to help them discover who they are in their innate nature; to build on their strengths, core values, interests, and passions.

Baillie: Yes, that's exactly it. In the current criminal justice system there's a lot of directive work. For example, youth may be required to attend classes on critical thinking, decision making, or victim awareness. Or, they could be assigned to work with a caseworker around finding housing or a job, which is great! Unfortunately, because of budget cuts and the restrictions of the workforce, there's not enough time spent listening to the young person, to enable them to think and mull over what's important to them – what they want – and that's critical. That's what coaching does. It provides a space for the young people to reflect and to be challenged, and also to provide championing when they need it.

Fran: To be seen and heard for who they really are. Yes, and to give them the opportunity to discover for themselves who they really are, underneath all those coping behaviors that they've had to develop for their survival.

Baillie: Yes, everyone's got their personas involved. For every young person, there's something that they're interested in and an identity that matches their values. Coaching enables someone to become whoever it is they want to be – not who their friends or the system wants them to be.

Fran: Is there anything else about your vision or your mission that you'd like to share?

Baillie: Yes, there are two things that distinguish our coaching approach from other programs associated with the criminal justice systems. First, it's a holistic approach. In the criminal justice world there's a term: "multiple and complex needs." Basically, for young people that end up in our sector, there's a lot going on in their lives. For example, they may not have a stable home to go to at night; there may be problems at home like domestic violence; perhaps they're not spending enough time with their families; or it could be mental health challenges, or drug dependencies; or all of the above and more. So there's a lot happening at the same time.

In typical programs, there may be a specific focus on a single issue area, for example, a young person's relationship with alcohol. In coaching we look at the person's whole life. So that enables us to work through those multiple and complex needs and the intersection between all of them. Then we can help them get targeted support once they learn for themselves what the underlying issues or drivers are. So that is really valuable, and a foundation for a lot of the other work that is going on in criminal justice.

> The coaching process leads to self-sufficiency.

The other piece that I really love about the coaching approach is that the coaching process leads to self-sufficiency. It helps people become independent in the long term.

Fran: Well put! Those are very clear – the holistic approach recognizing the whole person with their multiplicity of complex needs, uncovering the core issues and discovering the underlying drivers and their priorities for focus. And then there is the self-sufficiency piece. I appreciate that, too, because it's aligned with that old Confucius saying:

If you give a man a fish, you feed him for a day.
If you teach a man how to fish, you feed him for a lifetime.

Through the coaching approach you are helping them build capacity to resolve their own issues going forward. I am so happy you are out there doing this work.

Thank you, Baillie. Let's bring Lola into the conversation. Welcome Lola. What did you learn from your pilot coaching program?

Lola: We didn't put a lot of structure in from the start because we did not want to limit ourselves at the pilot phase. The young people in our pilot really took to the coaching quickly. We were surprised; we thought it might take a bit of time to build trust and for them to really grasp what coaching was, but I think it really spoke to the power of the coaching – that way of being with somebody who treats them with respect, that they took to it pretty much immediately. They got to experience people caring and really listening to them, helping them guide their own process, as opposed to telling them what to do. Respect is a really big thing and clearly they didn't feel respected in so many ways, and they really got to fully experience the respect that comes with being non-judgmental in the relationship with their coach. They also got to experience having the space and the time to reflect on their lives, which we all need. This was of huge benefit to them because their minds are extremely busy with the confusion and chaos that's going on in their world.

Fran: Good for you for building that trust so quickly. That's a reflection on who you were being for sure. How many youths did you have in your pilot program?

Lola: We had eight boys in our pilot program. We coached the boys for between one to six months while they were in custody, and then about one to six months when they were out in the community. Apart from the custody side, which is outside of our control mostly, the community time was very much directed by the young people. At that point they already had a relationship with their coach and they were calling the shots in terms of being mature enough to decide what they needed and when. We expected we would meet with them bi-weekly once they were out in the community, but sessions ended up occurring on more of a monthly basis.

What was really great about the pilot was how much we learned. We learned more about their world. As coaches, we're helping people raise awareness of their own world. In that process we are also raising our own awareness of their world, how they see their world and interact with their world. The boys felt an intense sense of overwhelm on release, especially in the first month out of custody. The criminal justice system imposes various requirements they need to meet, even though they are out of custody which after being institutionalized can be quite hard for them to motivate themselves to get to. Bearing that in mind, it was really heartening for us that most boys in our program wanted to continue the coaching on release.

Fran: Lola, what kind of requirements, for example?

Lola: There is a curfew between 7:00 a.m. and 7:00 p.m., which shortens their day. They may have to go and meet a probation officer or their Youth Offending Team. They have various meetings that they need to attend and if they don't make those they could be found to be in breach of their release license terms and they could go back to prison. When they first come out of prison their focus is very much, "I don't want to go back to prison." There are also adjustments they have to make, just because they have been so institutionalized. In custody, they have not been able to do pretty much anything without somebody's permission. They've not been able to walk out the door without somebody saying that it's okay for them to go out of that door. So genuine self-motivation is a big challenge for them, also because they were very under-stimulated in jail.

Fran: Lola, I'm so surprised that you didn't need to meet with them on a weekly or even more often than weekly basis. I'm amazed that once a month was enough. That is really surprising.

Lola: Yeah, it was a surprise to us as well. When we think about it – we're coaches, so we already think differently from most people. Not everybody is into intense growth like us. Growth is not easy; change is not easy. We know that we walk a path where being authentic and honoring our truth is really important to us, but we also know that the process of change is incredibly destructive. There is a whole lot of tearing down of old stories and thought patterns before you build up more authentic ones. And that's scary for anyone! I think it is respectful to really allow someone to go at their pace.

> There is a whole lot of tearing down of old stories and thought patterns before you build up more authentic ones.

Fran: What did the coaches appreciate about this experience personally?

127

Lola: I could tell you what my experience was as one of the coaches.

Fran: Okay, perfect.

Lola: I found the whole experience to be a massive privilege. With these teenage boys it's all about bravado. They are still relating to really old school ideals of masculinity, which doesn't tend to include being vulnerable and sharing yourself with another person. So to actually have them feel safe enough to let their guard down and share with me their dreams and feelings that they had never really spoken about before, and just knowing that you're the place they can come to, to talk about these meaningful aspects of their life, is an honor. They're not having these much-needed conversations with anyone else, but clearly are capable, and it's so good for them.

Fran: Now that your pilot is complete, what's next?

Baillie: We operate in London and Southeast England. Our plan is to stay in this area, as well as to reach out to different groups of young people. We're expanding in terms of the range of criminal justice exposure that our clients will have experienced. We started off at the back end, those coming out of prison, who are most seriously entrenched in criminal activity, and we're moving toward young people who are still involved in criminal activity, but less so, so that the work can be more preventative as well. We are expanding by gender, so we'll be working with boys and girls going forward and also expanding geographically within London and the Southeast. We've only worked with two Young Offenders Institutions, so we aim to work with a broader group of young people who come from different prisons and probation departments in the area. Ultimately we aim to extend nationally, but that will be a few years from now. We recognize that we will get young people who are at different stages of motivation to change, so we are thinking about developing targeted workshops that focus on specific challenges that young people have.

David Lockett, with PACT in Toronto, Canada has taken an active role in mentoring me. He shared the learning of PACT with Lola and me, so we have the benefit of their experience. And I am giving back to other programs in a similar way. There are several different coaching programs starting up across the United States, probably in other countries too, but I've been contacted by several in America and I'm taking the time to mentor them the same way that David has mentored me. So you know, his giveback is going even further and, ultimately, what we're trying to do at Spark Inside is just contribute to the body of knowledge on coaching people that come from more marginalized backgrounds, more disadvantaged backgrounds, so that coaches feel empowered and have the tools and training to not only coach in the corporate sector but also coach people who maybe can't afford the fees and who could benefit from the kind of transformation that coaching enables. So that's definitely happening.

Fran: So, you're about paying it forward and giving it back. I can see this expanding like sourdough as you grow, and raise awareness of the efficacy of bringing the coaching approach to working with youth at risk – expanding awareness and deepening the impact this will have in the community and society. I'm so inspired, Baillie, by who you're being, you and Lola, and your organization and your vision.

Baillie: Well, thank you. Can I share one quick story of the most emotional moment I've had with Spark Inside so far? I was in *a Canada Day* celebration, and I very randomly ran into the person that was leading our evaluation (our pilot program has been independently evaluated by the University of Cambridge). As an aside, the results showed that one year after Spark Inside's eight coaching clients had been released from prison, only one was reconvicted of a new offence and all were either pursuing or actively engaged in education, employment, or training. In the UK, the one-year national recidivism rate is 70% for young people leaving prison.

Anyway, I ran into the lead on the evaluation, and she told me that earlier that day she had a chat with one of our clients, a 16 year-old boy who had been in prison three times already. He had been released into the community, and he told her about his interest in working in a restaurant. The youth unemployment rate in the UK is quite high, so even a young person without a criminal record who has qualifications will struggle to get a job, and with a criminal record it's even harder. Our client said that he went up and down the street in the area where he lived asking every single restaurant for a job until he got one.

Fran: Wow!

Baillie: It really goes to show the power of coaching, that when people apply their drive and resourcefulness, and there's a real deep-rooted desire to achieve something, they can make it happen. And this young person – he had all of those skills already and he put himself out there. I think a lot of people would struggle to face that kind of rejection, but he kept going until he succeeded. And it really blew me away. So we learned through that experience and that of the other clients' success stories to manage our own limiting beliefs. You do want to be realistic, but we doubted this young person's ability to get a job, and he showed us that he could do it on his own.

Fran: Well, he obviously had direct access to a strength and the energy of his motivation and access to his resourcefulness, as you said. I have to believe that the coaching helped him get there and he did the rest.

Baillie: It was a matter of just understanding his identity and knocking down another door.

Fran: Yes. Once we get clear on our innate identity we have a whole different world view to operate from. Great work!

Steve Cessario

Interviewed by Fran Fisher April 11th, 2013.

Steven Cessario is the founder of CT Youth Mentoring & Coaching and creator of www.teenagesons.com. He is a sought-after mentor and coach for teenage boys, having eight years of in-depth experience with young people. Steven has spoken on various radio and TV shows, acting as a progressive voice to help parents understand their teen sons, and is credentialed by the State of Connecticut and Advanced Behavior Health.

contact@teenagesons.com
www.ctmentorandcoach.com
(860) 338-9856

Fran: Hi Steven! I have a sense that working with youth has been a calling for you. Is that right?

Steven: Yeah, it definitely has. I grew up in a challenging household where sometimes my ideas weren't necessarily accepted, and I just realized a few years ago that I was always searching for a mentor in some way. Once I finally found one, he encouraged me to move forward on my ideas and he really helped me choose what makes me happy. So yeah, I think it is my calling and some of my mentors think I have a natural gift to help people, so maybe my past has helped prepare me to help other people.

Fran: It's so interesting that you use those words because as I was listening to you I had written down the words "natural gift." Congratulations to you.

Steven: Thank you; thank you very much. Yeah, it's been quite a challenge, but it's very satisfying and pleasurable. So it has been well worth the struggles.

Fran: Beautiful. As you know, in terms of this book, I am looking for people who are bringing the coaching approach –

the paradigm, the skills, the tools – to working with youth-at-risk. Apparently you have stepped into this work drawing from your life experience without the formal coaching training, is that correct?

Steven: Yeah, that is correct. Over the past eight years, I have been involved with helping young people overcome difficult obstacles, and I have done that through the YMCA, high schools, and juvenile detention centers. I have been working with organizations where I have coordinated activities for mentoring young men. It just made sense to take my experience with working with young people and create an organization where I can help them on a larger scale and do it full time. My own mentor and coach also supervise me. So I do have an informal type of coaching and training. It is working and it is beneficial.

Fran: Well, the proof is in the pudding, as they say! You are making a positive difference, right?

Steven: Absolutely. My clients never really ask for my credentials. What really matters to them is that I can relate to them – that I understand them. I've been able to develop strategies to do that from my own experiences as a teenager. I clearly communicate that I'm here to help. I am not here to control them or tell them what to do. Really, trying to help them get to where they want to be – that's what makes them happy and successful.

Fran: That's absolutely the core of the coaching philosophy. So you are certainly operating in alignment with the empowerment model, aren't you?

Steven: Yes, I help them find that spark within themselves that they sometimes forget is there because of certain things like school. Sometimes school can be limiting for teenagers or youth in general. Sometimes parents are not aware school can be limiting for their children, and that is where I come in to help them become aware of what they can do to be more effective as parents.

Fran: So you work with parents as well?

Steven: When they ask me questions. If a client wants me to talk to them, I will. But it's mainly just about the client.

Fran: How is your program structured?

Steven: What is unique about my business is that I drive to peoples' houses, which makes it really convenient for parents.

Fran: So you basically work with clients one-on-one. When you are at their house and it's time to work with them, what are some of the important elements? How do you structure those times you are connecting with your client?

Steven: First of all, it's very important that I'm able to gain trust from my clients, and to create a supportive climate for discussion. I seek to develop trust by encouraging open two-way communications, which means sharing some personal experiences or just really getting to know them at first. I want my clients to realize that I am someone who'll listen, be encouraging, be open-minded, and treat them respectfully in the way they want to be treated. A lot of my clients tell me, "You know, my teachers, my parents, they treat me like a child and I want to be treated more like an adult." These are the years when they are becoming adults. Sometimes parents aren't effective with how they communicate their emotions or ideas or thoughts to their kids. My structure is creating openness and a climate for discussion. I provide listening and constructive feedback and advice. I help them with changing behaviors that are more appropriate.

Fran: Are the parents around when you're having these conversations?

Steven: It's a private discussion, so we sit somewhere in the house where the client is comfortable. The parents are usually in the house or they just run off for errands for the hour. Often the parents trust me enough that they'll feel comfortable enough to leave the house.

Fran: That is really cool. So the youth is in a familiar setting, which is safer for them.

Steven: Exactly.

Fran: Yeah, I can imagine having to go someplace else to meet with you. There would be more to overcome to build that trust.

Steven: Yeah, absolutely. They feel more comfortable in their own environment. It's safer. It's a lot more convenient for the parents as well, because they are really busy.

Fran: Do you require a minimum number of sessions?

Steven: I don't because I've come across a lot of parents who might be unemployed or might not have the financial means to pay for coaching. So I say to them, "It's still important to work with your son at least once a month." It's better than nothing, in my mind. In my experience, consistently meeting with a client is the best. The relationship is stronger. I see a bigger difference.

Fran: What else might be useful to share?

Steven: I believe adolescents and children, in general, really crave the attention of adults. My clients, who are teen boys, enjoy an adult who is encouraging and open to the things that interest them. Once they become comfortable with me, they're more likely to open up and share their feelings about the challenges that they may be having in their lives. And this makes coaching a lot easier.

Coaching motivates an individual to take on life. It is about challenging the client's thoughts to get to the next level they want to achieve. Discovering the client's desires is one step, and discussing how to get there is another. Helping them to believe that they can get to what they are envisioning is also

> I enjoy being challenged because it helps me think differently.

very important. I think my clients enjoy being challenged. Something that they say to me is, "I enjoy being challenged because it helps me think differently." That in itself – if I can achieve that with my clients, to help them think differently – is important to me.

Fran: Lovely. Beautifully said. "Motivated to take on life." This is a very special type of conversation they're having with you – calling them forth and finding strengths within themselves, isn't it?

Steven: Yeah, absolutely. Sometimes, the client doesn't have the support system at home where a parent is absent. Or a parent or sibling might call them names. They internalize and then they really do believe that they're selfish or they're stupid. All it really takes is for me to say, "I believe in you" or "I really liked what you wrote" if they are sharing a story or something. You know that is the important part about coaching as well: supporting them in the person of who they truly are.

Fran: Who they are, not who others want them to be.

Steven: Exactly, exactly, and I have come across a lot of parents who feel that what they believe is right. And they don't understand why their child doesn't take their advice. You know, parents tell me stories about how they were yelling at their son and screaming. So a lot of it is ineffective communication between the parent and child, which can strain the relationship. It can cause a child not to want to talk to their parents.

Fran: Do you have specific training regarding communication?

Steven: I was a counselor in college working with college students. I was trained in communicating with individuals. I also have gone through a lot of personal therapy as well. I have my own mentors and coaches who I work with weekly, so that's also training to me. It might be informal, but I am in constant research about understanding adolescents and masculinity and working with adults.

Fran: Thank you, Steven, for contributing an interview of one of your clients. I am including it here, with the questions I provided for you to ask him:

[*Steven describes the following client as*] "a bright teenager who is motivated to improve himself every day. He is very well-rounded and has a variety of interests, such as tennis, guitar, and biology. He is of Chinese descent and is now a sophomore in college. He has taken the strategies he learned working with me to cope with every day challenges."

When did you start working with Steve?

Client: The summer of 2012.

What were your circumstances/issues at that time?

Client: Teenage problems including college, grades, relationships, and setting goals.

Where were you spiritually, mentally, emotionally, physically at the time?

Client: I was relatively stable, but I felt sad sometimes and I needed an outside opinion.

What motivated you to work with a coach?

Client: The advice and the guidance they offered.

What did you want to accomplish? What was your top goal?

Client: I wanted to see where I was going in life and just try to relax about where I was in life. I wanted to be calm, but prepared.

What were your expectations about the process?

Client: There were no expectations; I honestly thought coaching does nothing.

What happened that you didn't expect?

Client: It actually helped. It gave me a lot of confidence and direction in my life!

How did working with the coach help you?

Client: My coach took the time to listen to me. He listened to my problems and gave me encouraging advice to sort my life out.

What did you learn about yourself?

Client: Life isn't perfect and sometimes life just happens.

How did you change your focus or direction?

Client: I still work hard but it's more passive; I just let it happen.

What obstacles, limiting beliefs, or adversities did you overcome to attain your goals?

Client: I got over the emotional barrier I had and this ridiculous belief that everything needed to happen exactly HOW I wanted it.

How did the process support you in overcoming the obstacles?

Client: It was the constant backup that allowed me to go forward whenever I would start to relapse. Plus, a person there to talk to about any issues in my life was enormously helpful.

What personal strengths helped you accomplish your goal or overcome obstacles?

Client: Mostly persistence and confidence in myself.

What changes and big wins did you experience as a result of working with your coach?

Client: The biggest was probably realizing that sometimes you just have to let it happen. Also getting over my breakup and talking through the aspects of my personal life.

How has your personal life changed? Work life?

Client: I have a more open mind in terms of relationships and a more humane work life.

What are you most proud of?

Client: My paradigm change and how far I've come.

What were your wins? Accomplishments?

Client: There weren't any wins per se, but I definitely managed to cheer myself up and look on the bright side of life. It's cliché, but completely true.

What were your breakdowns? Unmet expectations? Failures?

Client: I guess I still feel like I'm not too talented in anything. I still want to be good and a leader in a field of expertise.

What did you learn? How did you apply your learning?

Client: Basically everything I've listed above. It's part of my whole life; I love seeing my life in this new lens.

What is next for you?

Client: Off to college and just letting it happen. Whatever happens will happen.

What will you acknowledge your coach for?

Client: Steve has been an incredible human being. He is great at giving advice and listening. Even with some bullshit I've done such as missing the occasional meeting, he still remains patient and understanding. He tries to be there for me, whenever he can be. He's helped me come very far and I thank him for that.

Mark Demos

Interviewed by Fran Fisher February 27, 2013.

Mark R. Demos has worked with youth for 30 years. He created the Life Scene Investigation Positive Forensic process, which helps individuals discover their innate Talent DNA and Character Strengths. His programs have been used in mental health and by juvenile courts, school districts, and by coaches. Mark is about to launch the MyLifeScene digital experience in late 2014, to help teens and college students more accurately predict their future success and happiness using Positive Forensics, Big Data, and Predictive Success Analytics. Mark is the author of *The DNA Code: The Forensics of Purpose-Passion-Performance.*

www.mylifescene.com
http://m64019.wix.com/the-dna-code
mark.demos@corp-dna.com

Fran: Hello Mark! As a place to start, I'd love to hear about your background in working with youth.

Mark: Sure. I started working with youth many years ago, when I lived in South Africa. I worked with a youth program there for about six years.

Then in Seattle, I started a youth program in the late 1990s. I had spoken at a parenting group and they asked me if I did teen intensives. Turns out these are kids in rehab or just back from rehab that didn't do too well. So I started a rehab program virtually overnight. My sons were working with youth groups around Redmond, Washington, at the time.

So we started working with kids that were runaways. We'd find them and bring them back to their homes. We would get special orders to hold them. It was very intensive. I worked at these programs for about four years. We would tutor these kids, help them get their driver's licenses, and get jobs. One of my sons would help to do socialization stuff with the youth and get them jobs. It was a very intense life focus in getting these kids reengaged back to doing the regular things of life, but at the same time it was helping them change their perspective from "What's wrong with you?" to "What's right with you?"

These kids had been subjected to every sort of analysis, given labels, and then they lived them out from oppositional defiance disorder and a list of other negative diagnoses. They all had been diagnosed as ADD and ADHD. They would use that as an excuse before the judge: "I didn't know what I was doing." It was really ridiculous. It really was.

We would begin a redefinition of these kids. My model is really simple. It's really more from a sports coaching model. What I am looking for is evidence of talent: What is it that is hardwired into people that when they know what it is and they use it, it creates positive emotion?

I was asking questions like, "What is your talent? How do you engage in life in this academic environment? In terms of your social capacity, how do you connect with other teens or adults? Are you a leader, or are you a follower? What do you do? What is your function in your group? What do you have to give to your group?" We would look at Emotional Intelligence. We looked at a lot of the issues, like decision-making, for example. We recognized that issues like that are not fully developed, especially with teenage boys. We found out what is right. We helped them understand their history: "When did you connect? When did you make a good decision rather than bad decision?" We helped them start finding a good a pattern of good decision-making.

We essentially helped find what's right and how to repeat it; how do you develop it and how do you grow it?

And that is my model for coaching, especially for teens. One of the classic definitions of coaching is that the client is the expert. These kids have yet to engage in life, and so they are not expert in a lot, so we are helping them find out their

140

expertise in life – their unique capacities, so when they value them, they are less likely to do things that are harmful to their lives.

Fran: Spot on! What occurs to me is that this work is applicable to every teen, not just the ones that are at risk.

Mark: Absolutely. One of the programs we ran was with the Environmental and Adventure School in Kirkland, Washington. This was a very high-functioning junior high school campus. We taught the program for four years. This school was rated in the top ten by *U.S. News and World Report*. The kids attended for high school credit, and they absolutely loved the class.

Our goal was having the kids say, "This is who I am. This is what I possess, and, if this is who I am, this is what my future could look like if I develop and use these." Our model does have a very broad application. We find that a lot of the kids who have issues and have problems, primarily have an undefined life. Or, even if they know what their talents are, they misuse them.

A drug dealer on the high school campus is typically highly emotionally intelligent and highly intellectually intelligent. They know how to lead. They know how to create fear in kids' lives. Intellectually they know how to manage distribution. These are very bright people, but they contaminate the evidence – short lived in terms of how they use it, and many end up in jail.

Fran: Please say more – define what you mean by "contaminating the evidence."

Mark: One issue is wrong belief. We did a lot of work at Redmond High School near Seattle, Washington. These were wealthy kids and very often these kids believed they were entitled, that they were allowed more than others are allowed to do. They felt they were above the law. They had parents who would bail them out of everything, who would make excuses for them, who would find a diagnosis for them. They were given things they hadn't earned. They were seldom required to work or experience a sense of "I can be successful," because their parents stepped in all the time.

Another belief of contamination was "I am just not good enough." Someone told them they didn't have the evidence – that their belief about themselves needed to be changed.

In terms of human talent, it's not just for ourselves when we use it. When we grow we feel good. But, when talent is wasted, it leads to a lot of depression. The self-message is "I feel useless. I don't have the opportunity to use it. I have to dig myself out." Kids need to learn that they have the capacity.

> When talent is wasted, it leads to a lot of depression.

Also, another contamination of good evidence is the peer pressure for playing to the crowd. They are trying to make themselves look as if they are someone else. They need to be given the space to learn and discover. Trying to be bigger than you are, something that you are not, causes constant anxiety waiting to be found out. That's not very different for many adults, and it can be a powerful motivator with teenagers as well.

Fran: You help these kids to recognize the evidence that is a healthy and empowering view.

Mark: We do, and we do that from a number of perspectives. These kids are in school, and academics are a primary focus in their lives. We do some basic things that are very helpful. We look at learning styles that help them choose where to sit in class. Some are not looking at the teacher because they are auditory, so they are listening with their eyes closed, absorbing the information. Some kids are visual, sitting right in front, watching the teacher.

Here is a quick illustration. This was a teen in Dallas, Texas. She was out on school suspension because she was dealing drugs. One of the profiles we use in the schools is the VIA or Values in Action (www.viacharacter.org), and what came back was that she really loved learning. She stood up in front and said, "This test is a waste of time." One of her friends said, "What do you mean, saying this test is a waste of time?" Another friend said, "What do you mean, you hate learning? You are always reading magazines and looking at websites. You are always learning about chemicals and how to do make-up. You are always wanting to learn more." She applied her love of learning in ways that often in high school they don't like to look at because it is vocational and not academic – for some kids it's a waste of time to go to college. For them it will only cause frustration and anxiety.

Some vocations could even make more money than college graduates. Lady hairdressers and people who love doing hair can make a lot more money, for example.

Fran: And more fulfillment too.

Mark: Right. Exactly.

We also look at brain dominance, subject analysis, basic study skills; who am I academically, who am I intellectually (IQ); a lot of different measures helping them gather evidence: social, emotional, physical capacity, meaning and purpose, and spiritual capacity – all those areas to define and answer the question, "Who am I?"

Fran: Beautiful. You know this is a topic close to my heart. It is so important to discover our essential self.

Mark: Yes, and this year we started a program at a junior high school in Dallas, Texas, with 780 eighth grade kids. They are working with our curriculum three days a week for the next eight weeks for a total of 24 sessions. Next year the school will sponsor this program throughout the entire school year for both eighth and ninth grades, but at a far more in-depth level. We are starting to train the teachers in how to discover strengths. If a teacher can't find their own DNA Code of talents, how can we expect the students can learn to do it as well?

We are delivering seven hours of training and a whole lot of videos. We have the kids and the teachers do the Strengths Finder and the VIA. The parents will be encouraged to do the VIA as well. In order to help them understand the curriculum we will have 85 teachers, including the staff, janitors, and cafeteria workers. Everybody in the school is going to go through a short version of what we do in the curriculum. We take them through a short certification to help them become Life Scene Investigators to build their own lives, and then in two weeks' time we will begin with the kids. What we are doing in the school is pervasive. Then we will roll it out with a number of other schools.

Fran: Very exciting! It is a holistic approach, so that you can create a supportive environment for these kids. It's a design for success: creating the safety and support and environment where they can thrive and be held accountable, too, I am presuming.

Mark: Absolutely. As an example, the school has a TV channel for announcements. Every morning, at the beginning of the school day, there will be a one-minute broadcast with a teacher sharing their profile. In the classroom, each teacher has to begin the class by making a statement: "I am brave, I am creative..." using their Strengths Finder language – something about themselves. Then in the class, when a student stands up to answer a question, they have to first say, "My name is ___ and I am ___" (name a strength) before they answer a question. This procedure will be woven into everything in that school.

We are posting movie-size posters asking the question, "Who Are You?" in texting language, so it's a question mark and the letters: ? R U. It's going to be integrated through everything they do. They will have T-shirts they can wear and also small groups they can join. It's going to be a lot of fun.

Fran: I hope you have some research evaluators capturing the impact of all this.

Mark: Yes, we do. We ran a similar program in the Richardson School District here in Dallas with out-of-school suspension kids. These are kids that are dealing with drug charges, criminal charges, being a gang leader, or they brought guns to school, for example. We started two and a half years ago and we are having incredible success with these frequent flyer kids. These are kids that keep coming back repeatedly. We have measured a 70% drop in recidivism of these kids coming back. It's really cool to see what we have been able to do.

Now we are going to be rolling this out to 10–12 more schools in the next three years in this school district.

Fran: This is a model you want to see replicated all over the world, isn't it?

Mark: Absolutely. We are also currently developing a website, "My Life Scene," for kids who have been in our programs. Kids can post their profile, defining their lives with what is right. They can post a one- or two-minute video talking about themselves and their strengths. It's almost like an online resume, focusing on their areas of talent. Their teachers, friends, and even parents can leave a comment or a brief recommendation.

Fran: You have a magnificent vision, Mark. And you're living that vision. What a joy that must be for you!

Mark: Thanks. When we trained Teen Discovery in Seattle, a lot of our focus was kids that were on drugs. We'd hunt down these kids and find them around the country and bring them back to Seattle. We had incredible success with kids like that.

Heroin was the drug of choice for some of these areas. It is a really tough drug to deal with, and yet we are seeing some of those kids now married, starting families, or graduating college, because we really got in their face – not about what's wrong with them, but "Let's figure out what it is that, when you use it, it's going to give you what drugs give you." And what that is, is connection, and it is the experience of, "When I stand up, people notice me. I am emotionally alive and I know my place in the world."

We have the opportunity to develop this model in Costa Rica, Nicaragua, and Texas, as well. It is not just about healing and it's not just about the disease. It gets the youth hooked on the health of your unique design and your talents and using that to grow and develop, rather than always thinking, "I am just an addict." They get to redefine what and who they are, rather than something they are trying to avoid all the time.

> They get to redefine what and who they are, rather than something they are trying to avoid all the time.

Teenagers are growing and changing. There is a lot of life to help them discover and also give them discovery tools to help them discover for them themselves.

Fran: Are there any aspects of your program where you introduce a formal coach-client relationship to the mix? Do you have trained coaches working with kids on a regular basis? If so, what does that look like?

Mark: We have trained a lot of psychologists, counselors, and therapists. We have trained 70 here in a local Dallas school district, and an entire community mental health agency last year. We have trained a number in the Seattle area and LA Unified School District. One of the things we are doing at the moment is working with a university to create a curriculum for which teachers and therapists can get their college credit or coaching credit, depending if that is the route they want to go. We provide a 40-hour training program. This is a certification program for application in a coaching and facilitator environment and positive psychology interventions.

Again, my coaching model does differ somewhat. It's more what professional coaches would call consulting and mentoring. I come more from a sports coaching background, which has helped me in the process of discovering and developing talent. It's definitely more of a sports coaching model rather than a life coaching model.

Fran: So, you help a youth move through your curriculum successfully and you do that by bringing whatever particular support process that best serves them, whether it's consulting, mentoring, coaching, training, teaching, or counseling. Is that right?

Mark: It is. Yes. To me it's all coaching. I just see it's all coaching, because I'm taking them from one place and helping them get to another place, how to engage life from the platform of defined strengths. To me, identifying specific talents is the basis of coaching.

Fran: One of the core assumptions of coaching is that it is strengths-based. We help the client discover and build on their strengths.

Mark: I use what I call a forensic process to help people discover their strengths and talents. Each of our trained coaches brings their own life to that process – and their own strengths and capacities.

Fran: I'm curious because I am interviewing other organizations. I am seeing a variety of models, and there is some difference of opinion about how to involve the parents in your youth-at-risk program. So let's say you are working with an individual youth, to what extent or how do you include the parent in that process?

Mark: When we did the Teen Discovery Program, to me the parents were the primary focus. The parents were actually a bigger problem than the kids were. Parent coaching is vital. Parents are thinking about changing a kid because of a serious issue. We can get the kids to slow down and stop doing such destructive behaviors, but the parents were the ones we would focus on. The parents were constantly negative and wanted the kids to be something they were not or never would be. They would be pressured to not hang around certain kids. The parents always saw those kids are bad and their kids were wonderful. We would definitely work with the parents.

One of the programs here in Texas is working with the parents. They get a get-out-of-jail-free card if they attended our program, and the parents are required to attend. So we do a lot of interaction with the parents. We find the parents are the same profiles as the kids. We have redefined the teenager in the eyes of the parent. We coach the parent to treat these kids differently and to use language differently. We require certain boundaries because they need the freedom to grow into who they are.

It's vital to have the parents involved. Confidentiality is limited. It's not therapy. We are not working with a deficit model. We are teaching the parents the same skills we are teaching the kids.

We teach the parents to observe and learn about their kid's learning style. It's innate in their design and you know what makes them come alive when you observe them. When the parent learns to see what's right with their kid, the parent earns a lot more credibility with the kid.

Fran: My hat is off to you, Mark, for this work that you do!

Mark: Thanks. There is something else I want to mention. Once we teach the youth how to discover who they are, we encourage them to give it away. It's so primary for teenagers who have been so self-indulgent to realize they have something so vital – you've got to use it and give it away. We can help teens be less depressed. We can help them know they have talent and they can give it to this world. But, until they know what they have, they are anxious – they are uncertain. Knowing what you have and giving what you have is primary to anyone, youth especially. We encourage them to give it away at home, in the school cafeteria, anywhere, and keep on giving it because when you give it, you connect to other people and you learn more. So that to me is a primary focus.

I'd like to share one little caveat, Fran, before we wrap up, if I may.

Fran: Of course!

Mark: Around this time of year kids start talking about how to get a job for the summer. The first response that most teenaged kids have is it's so tough to get a job. So these kids – 80% minorities – are told you've got to go out and find a job, are out to find a job, and the very first obstacle they encounter is that they have to report that they have criminal convictions. If you look at any application, the first question at the top asks, "Have you ever been convicted of a crime?"

Most kids feel, "Why should I even continue working on this?" And most of them don't. So what do we do? We have a couple of sessions with these kids where we help them build a new resume for their job interview. We do the VIA character analysis and give them a little report from that. We tell them they are going to have new evidence – even for McDonald's.

Their resume can have a testimonial from a teacher or a counselor. We show the teachers how to do this. For example, "For the last 40 days (name) turned in his homework almost every time, showed up for class on time; he was respectful in my class." It is a witness statement form in which the kid can collect three to four of these and to include in their resume or at a job interview. They can say, "I've been convicted of a crime, *but* I am great at teamwork. I got caught breaking my curfew often, but I always turn up for band practice on time. I can't stand algebra, but I love creative writing." They give clear alternatives.

With this evidence, the kid can say, "I did this. This is who I am." It's really remarkable how this changes their view of life, instead of dealing with drugs or stealing to get what they want. Many end up in jail if they don't find a job. It's incredible how this gives them hope. And it gives us hope every time we do this.

It's hard, but there is a way through it. It's tangible. It's based on eyewitness evidence, rather than the youth having to beg, "Just give me a chance," which is highly unlikely.

Fran: And your point ties directly to the "Illusion of Hopelessness". You are in the business of busting up that illusion.

Jodi Sleeper-Triplett

Interviewed by Fran Fisher, October 28, 2013.

Jodi Sleeper-Triplett, MCC, SCAC, BCC, is the foremost expert on ADHD youth coaching. She is a master coach, speaker, trainer and author. Her company, JST Coaching (www.jstcoach.com), provides training programs to coaches, educators, and mental health professionals worldwide. Her first book, *Empowering Youth with ADHD* (2010), is the core of the JST Coaching training programs, and a highly acclaimed tool for parents and professionals alike. Jodi is an active member of the ICF, ADDA, CHADD, and ACO.

Fran: Hi Jodi, and thanks very much for being here. I'd love to hear about your special work with youth.

Jodi: Thanks, Fran. I started coaching young people specifically with ADHD back in the late 1990s. At that time, coaching – ADHD coaching – was just coming to the forefront. People were saying, "Wow, this could really be of benefit to adults," and what I learned very quickly when I got into coaching and explored the ADHD niche is that the adults with ADHD were all wondering, "What would my life have been like if I'd had a coach when I was younger?" So I decided to just go ahead and do it. And in all honesty, people thought I was nuts. They said, "You can't coach kids. There's no way you can. They will not understand it; they're not creative and resourceful." And I begged to differ with that.

And so I embarked on coaching young people with most of the focus being teenagers and young adults, although I do work with younger children face-to-face as well. But the interesting part for me is that what I've learned and experienced over all these years is that by bringing coaching to young people who have difficulties, whatever those might be – such as attention problems, focus issues, repetitive failures, problems with their social skills, or the tendency to engage in at-risk behaviors – those are the kids who really need the coaching. The benefit of connecting with someone outside of their family to talk to them about how they can succeed – what is it that's working for you, what's not working for you – and identifying the fact, which most of them never really knew until a coach explained to them, that ADHD is a neurobiological problem, not anyone's fault, and it gets in the way of focus, learning, and often basic skills, and that is one of the reasons they have difficulty in school, home, and even with friends.

There's also the tendency to do things before thinking about it. So it's the "act before you think" problem. And that often leads to the at-risk behavior in terms of drug and alcohol abuse. There is a huge problem – still – with self-medication for young people with ADHD. For the number of people in our prisons, youth detention centers, as well as adults in prison, I would say about 65% have some diagnosis of ADHD or learning disabilities. They were undiagnosed as kids, struggled, and went out and did whatever they felt they needed to do.

Fran: Oh, that is so sad.

Jodi: And got themselves in a mess. So my goal is try to catch them before that and to see what we can do to change – really change the picture for people who are out there struggling and not knowing that with proper help – whether that's medication, therapy, and coaching – or maybe not medication – that these young people do not need to end up behind bars.

Fran: You have stated this so clearly, Jodi. I love your mission to catch them ahead of the curve, so they can have a support structure in place.

Jodi: Yes.

Fran: And the learning to build new, healthier behaviors.

Jodi: It's such rewarding work as well. There have been many people I've helped whose families reached out to me afterwards with gratitude. I write back to them and say no, it was a gift to me to be able to do it, and that's still how I feel.

Fran: That's beautiful. I can hear how fulfilling this work is for you.

Jodi: Yes, I have an opportunity to work with the best and the brightest, and most of these kids – think about it, those who are at risk, they're survivors – they're so bright. Because how do you survive without skills and intelligence? Now of course some of their skills aren't the skills that you want them to be using; you know, breaking and entering and such.

Fran: Right.

Jodi: But in terms of learning and strategies and everything that they don't see as valuable, those are the skills that will get them far in life when we get them out of that negative or dangerous environment. But they don't get that unless they have someone on the outside saying, "Wow, do you realize that you have the skill set to succeed?"

Fran: I get that! Jodi, would you please share a success story of a youth you have worked with?

Jodi: I have one success story that I share quite often, and I have stories of those that didn't go so well. Occasionally, they go off, get help with what they need, and come back, which is great.

I worked with a young man who was 16 years old when we started. I will call him "Scott." He was a great kid, but struggling in school with learning issues with ADHD. Scott came to coaching independently and, fortunately, his parents were able to afford the coaching. We met on a weekly basis, checked in, worked using my coaching model on setting goals, using specific action steps every week to build the behavior and to create the structure, and to move toward success. We set up the plan for him and it worked really well. We had been coaching together for about six months when I got a phone call from him one day and he said, "Jodi, I owe you an apology."

Fran: Oh, interesting...

Jodi: "Okay, what for?" I asked, and he said, "Well I wasn't honest with you. I've been having trouble with substance abuse and I'm now getting help for that. My parents are aware of it and I've taken care of it." So that came right out of left field for me. I had no idea.

Fran: You had no clues or suspicions?

Jodi: No. That was one of my earlier experiences. He had never come to coaching on drugs, but it was something he was using for self-medication because it was calming. Most young people tell me it calms their brains. And if their brains are overactive and they can't sleep, they use drugs to sleep.

Fran: Oh, I see.

Jodi: And so, Scott shared that with me, and he asked if I would still be willing to be his coach. My response was, "I would love to help you move forward. My only questions, certainly, are: Are you committed to the treatment? Are you actively involved in the treatment program? Are your parents okay with this? And, is there anything else that I need to know in order for us to continue?" We made sure everything was good and we continued to work together. As it ended up, not only did he graduate from high school, he went on to attend a community college. We coached around different things through college, off and on, and then he said, "You know, I really want to go somewhere where I can be near the water. I want to surf." He was trying to decide where he would go and he picked a couple of schools here on the East Coast in the North Carolina and South Carolina area. Then he came to a coaching session and said, "Jodi, my big goal is to go to Hawaii. I would love to try to go to the University of Hawaii." I said, "Okay, what do you have to do?" He did what he had to do! So we ended up coaching while he walked the beach sometimes. He gave me the weather report in Hawaii, and I sat here in Virginia thinking, "Oh my gosh, I'm so proud of you!"

It was just amazing, the strides and the determination that came from this young man who originally thought, "I'll just get through high school," because that was it, it was like, "Okay, I made mistakes, I'm really not intelligent, I can't do this, I can't do that," and he's now gone through grad school. I think he is married now, and he has been working with inner-city youth up North. Scott is an amazing, amazing young man who I hear from only occasionally, because he is so busy. But to think that I had the opportunity to be a part of his life, and to have him say, "This coaching makes a difference." And to stick with me from the age of 16, off and on till he was around 20, that's huge for me. That was just such a heartwarming situation that could have gone the other way.

Fran: Congratulations.

Jodi: Thank you. They do it all and everybody thanks me, and sometimes I say, "No, no, no, no, you don't understand, I just provide the opportunity to have a safe space to explore."

> I just provide the opportunity to have a safe space to explore.

Fran: Well, he did the work, didn't he?

Jodi: He did. He worked so hard.

Fran: It's a testimony too, to having supportive parents.

Jodi: Yes, absolutely. That is so true. They're amazing people, and I was so impressed with how they handled everything. Sadly, I don't see that a lot in my world, because so many parents are frustrated and confused.

Fran: Yes, and they may not have the financial means to afford the coaching for their child. Some nonprofit organizations are working with kids in the inner city who don't even have parents. They are homeless. And funding is a big challenge for helping those kids too.

Jodi: Absolutely. A few years ago, the father of one of my clients created the Edge Foundation, which is a nonprofit organization set up to provide coaching to students, regardless of their economic means.

Fran: Fantastic.

Jodi: The problem of course is, sadly, these days it's so hard to get funding. But it's there – it's available. Every coach who is affiliated with the Edge Foundation has to have completed my Coach Training Program and additional Life Coaching

Training, so they all have a similar and aligned way of coaching.

Fran: That's wonderful, and would be a key to the success of the Edge Foundation, for sure.

Jodi: We've done research on it and it's all of that, put together to support the success. They've done some specific work in inner-city schools, and it has made a huge difference. But again, it's the funding challenge. When they find the funding, the opportunities are wonderful.

Fran: Jodi, what you have shared is an important contribution for this book. So I'm wondering, what else about your coaching approach would you like to tell me about working with youth?

Jodi: Well, I'll share it to you from two perspectives, one as a coach, and the other as the person who created the coaching model used in an ADHD coaching research study, which impacts all of this. First, as a coach, what I have learned is that it's extremely important for us to be consistent with the process. In life coaching, yes, whatever the client brings to the table is what we focus on. But, I find that being that open with youth can often create more of a difficulty for them than having a focus that we preset for them, knowing that there are times when we're not going to focus on that particular issue. So, for example, every client that I've ever worked with has what I call a Personal Coaching Agreement, so that we are working together at the beginning of the relationship to identify reasonable and attainable goals, but also setting up action steps. And those actions steps are very specific, like: What do you need to do when you wake up in the morning? What are your steps to move forward? How will you approach a particular issue or problem? What would your parents' involvement be if they were available on a day-to-day basis? How will you interact with me as your coach? We are really specific, so there's no guesswork, such as, "What did she mean – I'm supposed to touch base with her?" And then expect them to set it up. It's putting down very specific structure behind the coaching process.

Another piece is the incentive, the reward, especially in the ADHD coaching niche. We have youths who have never been able to really internalize the good feeling of doing something right, probably because many times people just tell them, "You're doing it wrong." So I wholeheartedly believe in positive reinforcement and rewards. Nothing major, but just something that's external to that individual to help them with their progress and their effort during the week.

Parents have to be able to understand that this isn't about getting an A. It's about actually sitting down and completing a paper or working toward that. It's about effort, not the letter grade or the amount of success. That's the big piece. It is having that structure around it and checking in on a regular basis. Now all the students know, they can come in with an issue. "I had a fight with my boyfriend or girlfriend" or "Wow, I just heard about this program that I want to enroll in. I don't know how to do that. What are the steps to take for that?" We still always have that core to come back to.

On the research side in the college realm, which has become a really big piece of the coaching world, the colleges now want to offer coaching to students on campus. What we did with the help of the Edge Foundation and a large grant was a two-year research study on coaching for college students with ADHD, and the end result of that was that each student improved in their skill level, their will, their self-regulation, and desire to move forward so they weren't stuck as much as they used to be because they felt: "Wow, you know, I am making some progress." At times it was a question of not managing themselves regarding making an impulsive decision, procrastinating, or choosing to do things that were not particularly in their best interest. They were learning to regulate their emotions and their decision-making process, and that's a big thing when it comes to the "at-risk" factor.

Fran: What a blessing it is to have the benefit of this research, so there are statistics to show this coaching approach is making a difference.

Jodi: Yes.

Fran: Awesome.

Jodi: It is very exciting. I cried when the research came out.

Fran: I would like to go back to this piece about positive reinforcement. Would you give me examples of the kinds of positive reinforcement that these youths have designed for themselves?

Jodi: Sure. Interestingly, these days, with everything electronic, oftentimes in order to succeed, these young people have realized, "I can't spend all my time either in front of a computer or on Facebook or phone or texting." So we shift it around so that they work on what's important for them to succeed in their lives. They turned it around and have Facebook or the phone or even hanging out with their friends as an incentive. They still get what they've had, but they've turned it around to earn it. They are working toward an opportunity to spend extra time with friends, some extra time on the computer, or being able to go out and do something. For families who have the means, we can use monetary rewards. It could be a dollar a day that adds up. A check-in could look like: "How did your day go? Were you able to follow through and take care of things? Great, we're going to put a dollar in the jar, and you go to the next level."

As they get older, later in high school, I find that money is one of the biggest incentives, but I also caution parents and grandparents that this is not about bribing; it's about the small carrot. What we do in the coaching, in setting up the incentives, is to look at the value of something they want. For example, an iPhone – it's not possible for you get an iPhone in a week, because an iPhone is very expensive and you need to work hard or have your effort sustained for a while. So what they do is come up with how many points or dollars would go toward that iPhone every week, knowing that maybe six to ten weeks from now they're going to get the iPhone. Having that daily and weekly tracking of their work, of what they're working toward, makes a big difference. What doesn't work – and it's fascinating – I've had kids who've been offered a car at the end of the semester or the end of the school year, and it makes no difference to them at all. They still fail. It's like, I'm never going to get there, so why should I try? And I've heard it over and over, and over and over.

Fran: More short-term or immediate reinforcement.

Jodi: Yes, they need that consistent, short-term reinforcement. So we can design it however they want it. With little children, they get stickers on a chart or in their assignment book, and now we're past the stickers, but we still want to have something that's tangible that they can see.

Fran: Yeah, and you learn that from trial and error, I'm sure.

Jodi: Absolutely.

Fran: And it's different for every individual too.

Jodi: I was in a meeting two months into the school year with an assistant principal at the school of one of my clients, the one who was incentivized to get a car at the end of the year. My client was having problems, and she looked him in the eye and she said, "I don't understand you. Your parents are willing to give you a car and you're not doing anything." And he said to her, "You don't get it. I'm never going to get the car; I can't get through today." I talked to his parents afterward and said, "This is what I was talking about before. Now you've heard it from your son's mouth. Can we change the plan?"

Fran: It's overwhelming; it's too big of a leap.

Jodi: Exactly.

Fran: Jodi, you are making a difference and it's fulfilling and rewarding for you. Youths are learning and parents are learning through the work that you're doing.

Jodi: Absolutely.

Fran: Youths are transforming the quality of their lives and the research is going to be published and it's going to raise awareness on a larger scale.

Jodi: Thanks. I believe I was put here to do this. This is my life and what I find really interesting is that I never dreamed that I would be travelling overseas doing this. I didn't expect to be working with hundreds of kids around the country, and now more around the world who are receiving coaching in this way. It's wonderful to be doing what I love.

Fran: Exactly, exactly. Job one is to be who you are, and you've been allowing this unfolding by honoring your vision, your mission, your values, and your strengths – being true to who you are, and look how this is unfolding so powerfully.

Jodi: Yeah, it really is.

Fran: What is your vision for the world of ADHD youth and adults?

Jodi: Well, on the coaching side, my vision and my mission is really to make sure that anyone who wants or needs a coach gets to work with one. I see coaching as a collaborative field and that anyone who thinks that they have to compete with another coach to get a client isn't opening their eyes to the needs out there, because we can be of service in so many ways.

For the ADHD community, my vision and my hope is that by doing this work we can help remove the stigma and provide opportunities for creating awareness through coaching for anyone who has a hidden disability. People walk down the streets and nobody knows what's going on in their brain. To help people with hidden disabilities to shine – to be who they were put on this earth to be, that's something that I see happening every day, and it's incredible.

Fran: Absolutely beautiful. And you used the word "hope," which is a key message in this book, showing that in every dark corner there is still hope, regardless of how anyone is viewing the circumstances.

Joe Cotton

Interviewed by Fran Fisher, December 3, 2012.

Joe Cotton is a Catholic lay minister who specializes in serving at-risk youth. His mission is centered on healing and empowering young people in need. Joe became a Certified Professional Coach (CPC) in 2005 and additionally holds a Masters in Pastoral Studies. Since 1999, he has served in parishes, schools, group homes, international orphanages, and juvenile detention centers. Joe is currently a youth minister in Seattle, WA.

www.stjames-cathedral.org/youthministry
jcotton@stjames-cathedral.org
(206) 264-2082

Fran: Hello Joe! Will you please share how you have been applying your coach training in working with youth at risk?

Joe: My pleasure, Fran! I completed my coach training and Living Your Vision® process at the Academy for Coach Training in Bellevue, Washington in 2005. Since then I attended the Seattle University Master's Degree Program in Pastoral Studies and I have been working in Pastoral Care ministries within the Archdiocese of Seattle.

Fran: All right! So you brought those two together: coaching and Pastoral Care Ministry.

Joe: Yes, I did. In 2007, I started as the director of the Catholic Chaplaincy for King County Juvenile Detention in Seattle, and I was also doing Catholic Chaplaincy at Echo Glen Children's Center in Snoqualmie WA, which is one of the state-run youth prison facilities in Washington State. I was in charge of running spiritual programming and providing spiritual services for young people who were incarcerated in both facilities. I brought a team of several volunteers through some training for providing Pastoral Care one-on-one. A lot of the principles between Pastoral Care and coaching are very similar and rooted in the same philosophies, so we were training all of our volunteers in these skills that were initially formed in me at the Academy for Coach Training.

We provided a lot of different services: Bible studies, church services, access to whatever spiritual resources the kids needed to support their spiritual needs while they were incarcerated. What I realized in doing that work was that the one-on-one conversations would provide a safe space for that young person to be able to tell their story, and to be able to tell their story in a way that was often-times a little bit more raw than they were used to sharing in other contexts. By virtue of being incarcerated, these kids were always in some level of crisis, and there was some level of clarity that arose when they found their freedom taken away. There was an instant clarity in terms of knowing what you want or don't want for your life. Our volunteers were providing a space for the young people so they could just start talking about that, and find a better understanding of what they were even going through.

Now I am in the process of writing for a grant to develop something for reentry for the youth, creating small group community services for when they come out of detention. I want to provide a mirror of the inside detention program on the outside.

Fran: I wish you great success for finding the funding you need for that program. It's so critical to provide that transitional support, isn't it? I am curious about what you see of the differences and similarities between the coaching and Pastoral Care.

Joe: Sure! Before I came to learn the art of coaching I had worked in group homes with at-risk kids and in the foster care system. I prided myself at the time for my good skills working with kids, but then I went to the Academy for Coach Training and it kind of ripped me apart a bit.

What I realized was that I was very good at lecturing kids and telling them what I thought they needed to hear – or what I thought they needed to be doing with their lives. I did a lot of talking at them, and I didn't do nearly as much listening. So coaching flipped everything upside down. All of a sudden it wasn't anything about my wisdom or me. It ceased to be all about me, and the coaching process flipped everything around and made me realize that they were the person with all of the wisdom and that they knew their own best solutions and pathways. My role wasn't to tell them what they needed, but to elicit what was already within them.

> My role wasn't to tell them what they needed, but to elicit what was already within them.

Fran: That was quite a revelation, wasn't it? And it sounds to me that as surprising or shocking as it was for you, your new awareness resonated deeply with you.

Joe: Yes! I remember struggling at first, because I was so used to giving advice and trying to solve problems. I think that's one of the pitfalls that people working with kids fall into. We move to advice giving or trying to fix their problems for them and make everything OK for them, and it's not a helpful approach. Coaching is all about holding them whole, capable, and resourceful. It is about helping them to access their own wisdom and develop their own plan. The results speak for themselves. Their likelihood for success skyrockets because it's coming from them.

Fran: That was a 180-degree mindset shift for you, wasn't it?

Joe: Yes. When I started studying Pastoral Care, I discovered that all of those things are exactly the same. Pastoral Care is all about listening and presence. Those are the two main parts to providing Pastoral Care. One of the fine differences is that coaching is a little bit more goal focused in terms of inviting a client to think about where they are now, where do they want to be, and how they want to get there – helping them to design their own plans for the goals they want to achieve.

There is an element of that in Pastoral Care, but Pastoral Care tends to deal more with internal woundedness, spiritual pains, and all of the stuff that the kids have been through. In Pastoral Care, we are looking at kids that have been physically, emotionally, and sexually abused, kids who are dealing with poverty issues, gangs, etc. They have been through quite a horrendous life experience by the time they get to us. So Pastoral Care is about providing a safe place where they can begin to talk about those wounds or talk about their lives. Pastoral Care is about sitting across from them, shutting up – which coaching also taught me to do – and really listening to what it is they are saying.

As with coaching, we are listening to what they are not saying, but still communicating. For example, what is their heart saying? What is really going on as they are telling their stories? The role of the Pastoral Care provider is to enter into whatever the person is experiencing. It could be immense pain or sorrow or loss. Our role is to actually enter into that pain or that scenario and not take it on as if it's our own, but experience with the person for a little while to feel what it feels like to be in that sorrow – to share it a little bit. In other words, to cut the burden in half. For the moment at least, there are two people sharing that difficulty. And the reverse is true. If the youth is sharing joy or happiness, we enter into that and experience the joy and happiness. In essence, we double the joy.

Fran: So you are saying that both coaching and Pastoral Care are about providing a safe space and deep listening, and that Pastoral Care training has taught you how to go deeper into the client's woundedness and pain with them. Is that right?

Joe: Yes, and that's kind of the presence piece, too. When the youth is telling me their sacred stories, where they have been, and what they have experienced, my entire job is to be a giant mirror, which coaching is also all about. It's about being a mirror for people to be able to see themselves, their true selves, their best selves, their ideal selves. Most people don't have those lenses on. For whatever reason, we struggle to see ourselves as amazing as we are, especially kids. Coaching is about seeing that about people, and recognizing and holding up that giant mirror and allowing people to see that for themselves, and then to move with that awareness.

The nitty-gritty skills that I would use are things like reflecting back, paraphrasing, or naming feelings. As they are sharing their stories I help them to name the feelings they are experiencing. In essence this is to help them understand themselves better than when they started meeting with us. Our job is to help them kick off the blinders. I used to say to the volunteers in their training, "You are going to hear horrible stories of abuse and horrible things these kids have gone through, and your heart is going to hurt and every fiber of your being is going to want to fix it. You are going to want to take away that pain. You are going to want to make it so the kid doesn't hurt anymore, and that is not our place. It's not our role and it's not helpful. Our role is to create a safe space where they can experience that pain, safely name it, identify it, and move through it." This way, somebody is sharing it as they are going through it, and we are helping them put words to their own experience, learn from their experience, and move through it so they can transform it into something good and blessed rather than transmitting it, which most kids in jail are doing.

For example, when a kid has a bad day at school and comes home all upset and they snap at their mom, they are transmitting their suffering from earlier in the day to their mom. Our job is to try to interrupt that transmission cycle and invite them into transformation, but the only way to do that is to really go down deep where they can touch those wounds, otherwise they'll spend their whole lives trying to escape that pain through angry behavior, abuse, alcohol, drugs, etc.

Fran: Do you have a specific client success story that you could share?

Joe: I have two stories I'll share. The second story will highlight a neat program that we started that was greatly related to coaching. In the first story you can kind of see the similarities and nuances between coaching and Pastoral Care.

The first one was a 16-year-old young man I will call "Brian." What was fascinating about Brian was that he avoided me like the plague. Most kids, when they are locked up, are very quick to come and talk to us. Often times it is boredom that drives them. There is not an awful lot going on when they are incarcerated, so they want to talk to people. When I walked into the unit I'd say hello. He would be polite, but he was always very clear he was not interested in meeting with the Chaplain. "Thanks, but no thanks." I always respected that; I never pushed or tried to convince him, but I continued to visit that unit and I would always greet him and smile. This went on for a couple of weeks, and then one day he told me, "OK, go ahead and call me and I'll talk to you." I pulled him out of the unit and took him to the library where we could chat, and we engaged in a conversation. I don't remember what we talked about in the first couple of sessions, but it was clearly two human beings getting acquainted and building trust.

After a couple of sessions there was enough of a bond of trust established that he started to tell his story. He was from a family with a single mom and ten or eleven kids. His mom was disabled and she was working a number of jobs to bring in enough resources to feed all of these kids. Brian was the oldest, and essentially was the other parent in the home. His life consisted of getting up early, waking up all his siblings, getting them dressed and fed, and making lunches, because the mom was already gone. After school it was the same thing. Other kids were shooting hoops, seeing movies, doing homework, while he was making dinner and helping his siblings with their homework. He did this gladly and graciously for a long time. Eventually what started to happen, even with his mom's number of jobs, she wasn't bringing in enough money for enough food, and they were chasing after bills all the time. He finally decided he had to do something to help support the family. He started busting into houses to get a few items to sell.

These stories unfolded over the course of four of five weeks and multiple sessions. He took me through the very first time he broke into a house. He shared how scared he was, but he just kept thinking, "I have to help somehow, survive somehow." He took me through how it got easier. As the minister/coach, what I am doing is just entering into feeling the anxiety with him, helping him name how scared he was, and reflecting back that it wasn't aligned with what he wanted, but that he felt it was what he had to do to survive. I reflected all this back to him, so he could gain a better understanding of what he had been experiencing.

As trust built and we continued to connect, I would sense there was something more there. As this story continued to unfold, I learned that he had a maternal grandfather – the family patriarch – who had essentially been his father figure. That man had died the year before, and this was enormously tragic for him. The amount of grief and loss, even a year later was palpable, once he started talking about it. That is where the spiritual pain was. He was experiencing such massive grief that he had never dealt with. He didn't have the luxury of grieving, given all his responsibilities.

Then the spiritual care became listening to all his stories about his grandfather and what his grandfather had done for him. Finally, for the first time, he was touching the pain that was connected with the loss of this man. He shared how alone he felt and how overwhelmed with the additional responsibilities that fell on him after his grandfather died. We literally spent our time crying together, mourning that loss together and moving through that pain.

Meanwhile, as our meeting times continued, I heard about his girlfriend, a relationship that was life-giving to him. Then he realized he did have some anger and resentment about all these responsibilities. He was missing school dances and school sports, and had guilt for feeling those feelings. He believed he was a horrible person that he was angry about these adult responsibilities. As his spiritual provider, my job was to let him know that it was OK to feel angry – to recognize that it is an unjust situation for a 16-year-old to be in, and to allow himself to feel those feelings.

So in the end, he had invited me into the most vulnerable, most sacred parts of who he was and together we touched the pain and we shared in the joy. We cried and we laughed together, and this was the kid

> All I was doing was creating a safe space for him to simply be who he was – totally raw.

that didn't want anything to do with me. This beautiful relationship developed and all I was doing was creating a safe space for him to simply be who he was – totally raw. I saw all the ugliness, and all of the beauty, and the whole thing was astoundingly beautiful. In reflecting what an extraordinary human being he was, he got to see that in himself.

That's Pastoral Care. It is being present and really listening and helping them understand their experience and their pain.

Fran: Congratulations! That is a wonderful success story, and illustration of the depth of your listening.

Joe: Thanks. Here is the second success story. One of my college colleagues created a program called MAP (My Action Plan), and I chuckled, because this reminded me of what I experienced with the Living Your Vision® process in the Academy for Coach Training curriculum.

We wanted to bear witness to the clarity that kids had about what they wanted and didn't want. Typically, as soon as they got out of incarceration, that clarity went away. This program was designed to capture that clarity when it was surfacing and produce something tangible. Our volunteers would meet one-on-one with kids, and it was all the same coaching principles at play: Everyone is whole, capable, and resourceful; eliciting their wisdom; helping them to identify their own solutions.

We created a process for them to identify what they wanted for their lives, what actions they wanted to take, what activities they wanted to engage in/not engage in, and brainstorm the people who could support them and other resources they would need. The whole thing was written down and put into a binder with their name on it. It was their plan and they did a lot of the writing. They walked out of detention with this binder.

We piloted the program, and the first kid we worked with was "Sam." He was about age 13 and one of our "frequent flyers." Frequent flyers are what we call kids who keep coming back. Sam couldn't pull himself out of that cycle, so we got to know him really well. When I sat down with him to show him his own finished product, his whole body changed. A light came on and this glow came out and his smile came through. It was very much like the process of coaching, where we created the space for him to access his own wisdom and solutions. You could just see how excited he was sharing this with me. We were high fivin'!

Anyway, we lost track of Sam after he was released from Echo Glen, and we were praying that he was doing well.

Some of the kids leaving Echo Glen were not going straight home, but being funneled into a middle point group home. My partner who works with me in this re-entry program lives close by one of those homes. She made some connections, got permission to do some reentry stuff with the kids in that group home, and sure enough, there was Sam! She found out that somewhere in transition, his MAP had been lost. So, she took a copy of Sam's MAP, went back to that group home, and sat down with him. She described his reaction to seeing his MAP again. He was amazed and re-engaged! Now he is on our first youth mission team and he is beginning to engage in doing community service. He likes it that he is being a pioneer in our pilot program.

Fran: I can hear your energy, enthusiasm, your passion — your excitement seeing the light bulbs go on. Congratulations!

Joe: That's where the passion comes from for me. Now, I am starting to launch a re-entry program, and we are trying ways of working with kids as they are coming out that will provide a community of support. We want to put formerly incarcerated kids in local community programs that are mission focused and support them at the same time in discovering their own life mission or life purpose, especially one that is rooted in their gifts or talents and how they can be of service in the world. We want them to discover what gift they have that the world needs, and then the team gets to pool their talents and come up with some service projects — something that is important to them.

Fran: You are so dedicated to supporting these youth at risk in moving beyond "risk" to enjoying healthy, productive, contributing lives, aren't you? How has this work changed your life, Joe?

Joe: Fran, it has deepened me. When you are working with at-risk kids, especially incarcerated youth, people are concerned about you becoming embittered. That hasn't happened for me. Doing this work, it does break me apart, because my job is to enter into the suffering of other people. That does get hard. There is a certain level of weariness when I do that. But what I have found is that if I allow my heart to break along with whatever the pain I am encountering, it is making space. It opens up room, and God's love fills those broken spaces and it makes my heart bigger. My heart expands. My heart breaks almost like it is bleeding love, and that love is filling into those spaces that I have opening up. It makes me better able to respond with compassion and understanding. It helps me to continue to remove all judgments from my presence, because if I am ever working with anyone and there is a hint of judgment, they are going to run for the hills. That's how I have found it has affected me. There is something authentic that is happening to me that when I am sitting across from these guys, even if they have never met me before, somehow they know I am a safe guy to be real with and they will let their barriers down.

> God's love fills those broken spaces and it makes my heart bigger.

Fran: Joe, how do you manage your self-care?

Joe: Self-care is probably the most important thing I need to attend to. It's the little things like getting enough sleep, eating right, and attending to my own personal relationships.

That is of the utmost importance, because otherwise I will burn out.

I have learned that at the end of the day I need to take the awfulness that I have encountered and give it back to God. I say to myself, "This has been mine to carry, and I've carried it for a while, but I can't take this on, because it would break me if I took it all on." I gratefully give it back to God, and I say, "You are big enough to hold this. I am going to go home, watch TV, and go to bed."

Fran: Good for you and it sounds like that is working. That's beautiful, Joe. I am curious, you mentioned earlier about your Living Your Vision® experience, which was part of your Academy for Coach training. How well have you kept your personal Living Your Vision® statements alive since 2005?

Joe: I have kept alive the part of my Vision Statement that declares, "I am a compassionate, playful, goofball that cares deeply and loves tenderly." That has stuck with me over the years. I am always the guy that wants to play, not as a class clown, but more about enjoying life to the fullest – never taking things too seriously, and that has served me well in working with teenagers.

Fran: That is SO you! That is how I knew you then and it is wonderful to see how you have brought your authentic presence into your work with youth-at-risk. Also, thanks for sharing this following testimonial from one of your clients. It is a tribute to the fruits of blending the elements of coaching and Pastoral Care into your work.

Reflections from "David," a Detention Inmate

David was a frequent flyer that was continually in and out of detention. He was a 17-year old caucasian young man who struggled heavily with drug and alcohol addiction and he frequently served time for drug-related crimes. David was an extremely cheerful person. He would greet you with a huge smile and authentic warmth, the type of kid whose mere presence would light up a room. He exuded deep goodness as a human being. He was funny, intelligent, and generous, although he saw none of this in himself. Behind his cheerful disposition he carried deep wounds, including a horrible self-esteem and self-image. Drugs and alcohol covered his pain.

"I am writing this from inside a cell in the King County Juvenile Detention Center. As you can imagine, it is not the best place for a 17-year-old kid to spend his days. Most times, I get very depressed and lonely. All I can wish for is someone to talk to who won't judge me or think I'm a bad person, someone who will just listen to me when I need to talk. The Chaplains here provide all this and more. They give me a release from my own negative thoughts. I believe that the Chaplains help kids more than any other program this place provides. They always remember me and have nice things to say to me when we see each other. I can tell that they put huge effort into changing kids' lives for the better. They do many things to cheer us up. They talk to me from an understanding point of view and I feel a strong connection with most of them. I think that my time here would be much more difficult to handle without the Chaplains being available."

Reuel Hunt

Interviewed by Fran Fisher, April 16, 2014.

Reuel Hunt is a passionate pioneer of the coaching profession. He has taken a simple coaching approach and taught hundreds of inmates the value of coaching. His latest program, Dignity for the Prison Population, is focused on empowering the entire prison population, including guards, executives, staff, and inmates. He is the voice of the unseen and unheard in prison.

(303) 734-0444

Fran: Hello, Reuel. I'd love to hear about the work that you're doing, bringing the coaching approach to working with youth. How about starting with your background and how you got to where you are now?

Reuel: Okay, I'll start with the story of my son, who is in prison. His mother and I divorced when he was three and he lived with his stepfather for 10 years. At the end of 10 years he called me and said that he had been beaten with a baseball bat. When he was apart from me, I was in the corporate world and I was – I guess I was just too busy to notice. I knew something was wrong, but I was living in Chicago and he was living in Dallas. I would get time with him for a year or two and know something was wrong, but not know what. I wasn't curious back then; I just let it go. Then I learned that he'd been beaten for 10 years.

My son was put into a mental institution to keep him from being out of control – where they tied him to a bed for 30 hours with a net. He was a drug addict at age 13. Once he was in a hospital for an overdose and he was beaten unconscious. He is currently in prison, serving 4–8 years for attempted murder, but being put in prison has actually saved his life.

It's sad that he was beaten; it was sad that he went through those 10 years of being beaten and me not knowing what to do. He is now recovering and he's doing well. He is going to school in prison and he may be getting out soon.

So, his life drew me out of the corporate world and into coaching. I was searching for something that would work, and I found coaching in 1996.

Fran: It sounds like finding coaching saved your life too!

Reuel: Yeah, and I didn't know it would work at first. I found coaching sort of parallel, I guess, to my working with him and all the systems that didn't work. I started a hotline in 1997, so when kids got into trouble, they could call the hotline. But I couldn't find services; there weren't services available. So there was no need of having a hotline if you couldn't find services.

Fran: Oh, I get it. You recognized the need for supporting kids in trouble, but you needed services to refer these kids to that would provide the services they needed.

Reuel: Yeah, in 1999 I started looking around and then in 2000 I found the Coaches Training Institute (CTI), and their Prison Project in Colorado. This was a program where they taught inmates coaching skills. They had a program called Jericho Road that trained inmates to be coaches, and they were coaching teens and their parents from the Juvenile Justice System. The inmates were being sentenced to this program in the Federal Prison by judges, to go out and be coached by the inmates for two hours, once a week for 12 weeks. It was transforming these kids and the parents.

Fran: So this was happening in your own backyard!

Reuel: Yeah! So, I met the people at CTI and we fell in love with each other and the journey began. We partnered up and became the Bigger Game Prison Project. We delivered 26 weekends in the Federal prison, and that was the start of the program.

Fran: Where did the funding come from?

Reuel: We wrote grants and Laura Whitworth did The Bigger Game workshops – one in California and one in Denver, and we raised $100,000.

Fran: Fantastic.

Reuel: And that was the beginning of Coaching Kids, Inc.

Fran: Coaching Kids, Inc. – was that your company or was it a collaborative?

Reuel: It was the nonprofit that we started that is still going on. We are doing work in the Oklahoma Women's Prison and in the Colorado Women's Prison. Laura separated from us in 2004. She took her project and changed the name to Time to Change, but it did not do anything. We took back the program. It was 2006 when Laura died, so we started a program in Women's Prison called the Laura Whitworth Prison Project. We got permission from her for this just before she died. And we did that for a couple of years.

All along we were doing programs in schools, in churches, and other nonprofit organizations. For example, we delivered a program called Girls Inc. in Los Angeles, Seattle, Philadelphia, and Denver. We were doing lots of work with youth, teaching a mini version of an introduction to coaching skills. We were teaching the basics of listening with powerful questions, coming from curiosity without judgment, and using your intuition. Other key pieces were values and saboteurs, perspectives, and action and accountability.

We delivered six two-hour modules, so we could deliver it in a total of 12 hours. In the prisons it took more time.

Fran: Very good. So it sounds like your work evolved from working with adults in the prison project to working with kids in the juvenile system in prison, as well as in public and private schools. Is that right?

Reuel: Public and private schools and nonprofits like Girl's Inc., which was an after-school program for girls. Yes, it was all about teaching coaching skills.

Fran: Reuel, as you look back, what difference did this make for the individuals you were training in these basic coaching skills?

Reuel: The difference it made with the kids – they are going so fast – it made them stop and think and listen. And the biggest thing that happened was that they would see a change in the other child while they were coaching them; the "aha" moment, the wake up moment, the "oh, now I see" moment that the kids would have in their triad.

Fran: That's amazing.

Reuel: Yup! Listening to each other and observing the coach – yeah! They got to have the experience of being heard. The coaching gave them a chance to be heard. We were doing twelve-minute coaching exercises back then, but now we are doing four minutes. We

> They got to have the experience of being heard.

do four-minute triads. I know, it doesn't seem like much, but it really gets to the core fast.

Fran: Fascinating. I am curious to know if you have been able to check back – like a follow-up – a year or two later to see how much of their experience has been retained?

Reuel: We haven't – we haven't had the funding for a tracking system. We didn't realize at first that you needed to really focus on that.

Fran: Sure.

Reuel: I mean – it's really hard to keep track of them.

Fran: That's understandable.

Reuel: We had a grant written that included follow-up tracking, but we didn't get that grant. We just hadn't had the funding for it. We know that tracking gets money, but we are not about money, we are about making a difference. And we run on a shoestring training, but we have been up in Oklahoma every month now for almost four years, once a month, every month. I am teaching in Oklahoma and I am teaching in Colorado, and I still fly back and forth.

Fran: What have you been doing in Oklahoma for the last four years?

Reuel: We've been training women in prison, and these women are – they are childlike. Oklahoma has more women in prison than anywhere else in the world – twice the national average. Did you know that?

Fran: No, that's serious – and curious.

Reuel: Yeah and it is because Oklahoma is so conservative. They are ultraconservative.

Fran: Who is "they?"

Reuel: The government, the population, and the culture. Tough on crime is their big focus now.

Fran: Okay. Tell me about working with these women in prison – how are you doing that? How is that going? And why do you say, "They are childlike?"

Reuel: It's going well; we are working with six women. One was in my very first class. Two others came right after that and they are now trained to be trainers. So they know the stuff inside and out, and they teach it. So, for example, this past January, February, and March, we trained three sets of people in four days each.

Fran: That's terrific. I imagine having them training their peers is quite a success factor for your desired outcomes.

Reuel: Yeah, people are getting out of prison all the time and they come back into our communities and, you know, people say, "Oh these people are going to get out one of these days." No, they are getting out right now, and they come back to the community and work. And they are childlike and unprepared for what they are walking into. They end up re-cycling back into the system because they aren't prepared for what they're facing.

Fran: How does the coaching training prepare them for adjusting to the outside world?

Reuel: It has them stop and look at their lives and look at themselves and look at where they're going. It has them see in other people what they can't see in themselves, and then they see it in themselves. When they are in the triads, they hear other people being heard – like they can just listen with curiosity, without judgment – and they hear them wake up, get an "aha" moment, and they move forward.

This last time when I was down there I talked to one girl who – I don't know the entire story – but she had five kids, she was 24 years old, and she got divorced. She was smoking weed, but she was a good mother – and suddenly she's in prison for having drugs and her kids are scattered here and yonder. She went from – I mean in a year's time – she went suicidal, cutting her arm. She had cuts all over her arms. She volunteered and I coached her and she had an "aha" moment, but it took 40 minutes. I was going to do a ten-minute demo, but it lasted 40 minutes. There wasn't a dry eye in the house. She had a breakthrough and now she has written to find out about her kids. It is pretty marvelous – transformational, actually.

Fran: Oh, it's so touching. She's starting to take back her personal power.

Reuel: Yeah, exactly. As a matter of fact, we have added two new modules, "Who is Driving Your Bus?" and "Who's Got Your Power?"

Fran: That's wonderful work you are doing, Reuel. Will you please tell me another success story of a woman in your Oklahoma prison program? And, what were her key issues when you started?

Reuel: We had a woman who had lived on a farm. She was married with four sons. She was driving under the influence of alcohol when she had a crash and killed her oldest son, his fiancée, and her friend. She was the only one that survived and she was in a coma for three months. When she woke up, they put her in prison for driving and drinking and killing someone. So, when I first started working with her in the class, I did a demo coaching with her as my client. We were doing a coaching on perspectives – and we were going somewhere else when I said, "This is not quite the issue." And then we got to it. She really wanted to commit suicide. She did not know why she was here. She wanted to be dead with her son. I had to physically move her out of that perspective and move her to another perspective. Geography is very important. We got her all the way around to being the mother of her other three sons – her surviving sons, and being their mother.

Fran: Will you explain what you mean about "geography"? What does that mean?

Reuel: Well, we physically moved around a circle that represented different perspectives on her issue. She started in the place that represented her current perspective. Then I physically walked over and moved her – she wouldn't move, so I moved her over to another place to stand. And you could feel the whole room change.

Fran: Did she come up with a different perspective in that different space?

Reuel: At first she couldn't come up with any; she could not get out of her current perspective. I mentioned a few possibilities and moved her into those different perspectives, and then she finally came up with, "Well, I can be a mother to my three sons." We got to it slowly. I asked her, "What do you want?" And she blurted out, "I want to talk to my three sons." And I asked, "What will you say to them?" And I said, "You have to be the mother." And she said, "I have to be the mother to them, don't I?" And I said, "Yeah."

Fran: That's a huge shift.

Reuel: A huge shift – yeah. She had been very quiet up to that point, and for the rest of the day, she was very talkative.

Fran: Wow, she had a release.

Reuel: Yeah, she did – yeah – yeah.

Fran: How has this work changed your life?

Reuel: Well it goes back – you know, if you go all the way back to when I was in the corporate world, I was in accounting. I was an Accounting Controls Manager, and I had a lot of responsibility. I wasn't a typical corporate guy, but I was very busy and I didn't stop to smell the roses. I wasn't curious. I wasn't focused on me first. I wasn't focused on taking care of me to take care of you.

Fran: How has this coaching work changed you?

Reuel: I have to take care of me first. I was doing that, but it was from the ego; it was for phony me, not the real me. It was for the persona of me. And now I'm focused on what I can do. As I focus on what I can do for others, I notice that there's a real focus back on me.

Fran: How does that work? It sounds sort of paradoxical.

Reuel: It does, doesn't it? Yeah, it is a paradox. Yeah. As I'm doing all this, as I'm in the middle of it, running in the background is the calm collected me at work, doing what I love to do.

Fran: Ah. And what you love to do is be in service to others?

Reuel: Yeah, um-hmm. Yeah.

Fran: So you're feeding that value of service, and I dare say Reuel, you're now feeding your soul.

Reuel: Yeah.

Fran: Yeah, and now the other thing – may I offer my intuition?

Reuel: Sure.

Fran: When you are doing for others, you are fulfilled by who you are being. And you're conscious of the fact that it's who you're being that empowers you to do what you're doing?

Reuel: Yes, exactly.

Fran: So you love what you do, and you're doing it and you're doing it on a shoe string. What is your vision for the future of your work?

Reuel: Well, in 2005 I wrote a two-page ten-year vision statement and that's coming true next August.

Fran: Oh my gosh! I love that. Congratulations!

Reuel: Yes, and it's very big. I just revisited it. The women in prison in Oklahoma have been asking me for it for four years, and I read it to them this last time. And it's the first time I had read it in a couple years, and I said, "Oh man! I need to get busy, don't I?" Because I've got my programs in several countries and throughout the US and I am not nearly there. And you know, I had a mini stroke last November, but I am gearing up, so look out!

Fran: All right, I believe you.

Reuel: I don't know how it happened, but it just – what I noticed is – if you have an intention and you just show up and do what's your share and consciously let others do what they do, the universe has a way of getting you what you need when you need it.

Fran: I am reminded of a Sanskrit mantra, Om Bartanam Nama. Translated it means, "I nourish the universe and the universe nourishes me." I hear you saying that you do your unique part and the universe rises up to meet you.

Reuel: Right. Meets and exceeds. And my son may be getting out soon.

Fran: Well that would be part of the miracle too, wouldn't it?

Reuel: Yeah it would be – yeah. We work with 15 or so every month in these women's prisons. That's not even a cup in a bucket, you know. I do feel urgency. I think there are 200 a month that are released in Oklahoma and in Colorado, and my vision is to help them prepare, so they don't come back.

Fran: Beautiful, beautiful. I commend you for the contribution that you're making, Reuel. Truly astounding.

Reuel: Thanks.

The Mockingbird Society

Jim Theofelis interviewed by Fran Fisher, October 8, 2014.

The Mockingbird Society is a nonprofit organization based in Seattle that serves children, youth, and families involved in the child welfare system throughout Washington State and the nation. Through their nationally recognized programs, The Mockingbird Society is committed to working collaboratively with youth, families, and community partners for system reform and improvement. The Mockingbird Society works with young people and families to build a world-class foster care system and end youth homelessness. The Society trains youth who have experienced foster care and homelessness to be their own best advocates so we can change the policies and perceptions that stand in the way of every child having a safe and stable home.

Jim Theofelis, Founder and Executive Director
jim@mockingbirdsociety.org
j.theofelis@gmail.com
www.mockingbirdsociety.org
(206) 323-5347

Fran: Hello Jim. You founded The Mockingbird Society in 2000. I am intrigued, what's the story behind the name you chose for your organization?

Jim: I named the organization The Mockingbird Society after the American classic, *To Kill a Mockingbird*, by Harper Lee. I was always touched by that story even as a young child. And for me, one of the themes that got me the most in terms of social justice was the notion that the characters who seemed to be the leaders and the pillars of the community at the beginning of the story, as time went on, I noticed how that slipped. Later on in the story, many of those community leaders were the same ones who wanted to lynch a man, not necessarily because he was guilty, but because he was black and had gotten accused of some horrible crimes. Those were the people who were now out of control, breaking the law.

Also, at the beginning of the story, those who were introduced as the scary ones, like Boo Radley; they ended up being the heroes. For example, there is a scene in the story when Boo Radley came out and picked up the child and protected him, becoming an unexpected hero. And then, of course, there's Atticus. For me it wasn't a direct reflection of me necessarily seeing myself in Atticus, but really the Atticus in all of us who could be the humble leader – not only strong in the light of day, but also in the face of critical adversity. I learned a lot about leadership from that book.

Fran: Well, Jim, I see that you have manifested a movement for social justice for youth, calling on those principles of leadership that you learned as a child, reading that book.

As you know, I attended your Eighth Annual Benefit Luncheon in September and I was deeply inspired by your vision, your mission, and the growth and success of your organization since 2000. What was your inspiration for founding The Mockingbird Society?

Jim: Well, it came from 25 years of working on the streets with young people as an outreach worker, working as a counselor, working as a director of several group homes and as the director of the Mental Health Clinic at the local Juvenile Detention Center. Over those years, I was seeing a distinct pattern where kids were making some questionable and even really bad choices, but I also looked at their behavior – not as who they were in the moment as much as communication from them about what was going on in their lives. So when one youngster was wiping feces all over the group home wall and I got called in to conduct a clinical consultation and the staff wanted to kick the kid out and raise his meds, I started with, "This is about communication. This kid is telling us his life is a bunch of poop."

I saw how kids were blamed and shamed for expressing the pain of the trauma that they had experienced as children. My first question is not so much how to punish or "fix" this behavior but rather "what is this child telling us?" I mean, that's a terrible mess – nobody wants feces all over the walls – but I was convinced even back then as a young professional that more medication and more restriction and more blaming and more punishment was probably not what this child needed at that moment and, in fact, it will probably not get the staff where they want to get with this child.

The other dynamic I was aware of was how hard young people and families work to overcome what life had given them, but also what they faced in trying to navigate systems – whether it was the Child Welfare System, Juvenile Justice, Mental Health, or even the school system. And how hard folks tried, but no matter what, the systems' dysfunction was even more powerful than their own ability to navigate the maze of systemic policies, practices, program eligibility, and of course, the often inconsistent professional staff interpretation of each of these programs, policies etc.

For example, one of the key issues that I wanted to address in founding The Mockingbird Society was the policy that any youth who achieved a high school diploma/GED and turned age 18 was ineligible for foster care that same day. This was true across the country and certainly here in the State of Washington. We had kids in our system who were born into foster care and some had as many as 25 different placements. As adolescents, some of them might have spent some time on the streets. All of this crazy trauma and then they finally managed to get a high school diploma and their reward for that was they're homeless the very next day. It's the reason I would call the foster care system the "gateway system to homelessness". We had counselors, foster parents, state social workers advising some youth NOT to earn that high school diploma or GED because we knew the youngster would be literally homeless the next day. Those are the kind of policies that I refer to when I say that no matter how hard a youngster works, there were just some crummy policies and practices in the systems that really make it hard to break out of foster care and start their adult life on equal footing with their peers from healthy families.

So I created The Mockingbird Society to address two urgent issues: One, watching how the system did not have the capacity or the patience or the energy to look at children not as a set of behavior problems, a diagnosis, and something to be fixed, but rather as a child who has experienced horrific trauma and neglect both prior to and after entering the foster care system. That's one piece of it. Two, at the systemic level, just how crazy making it was for families and kids trying to get to the next best place and how sometimes it was the system itself that created more drama and trauma.

We've got one youth here at Mockingbird today who was in 35 different foster homes. He was born into foster care with cocaine in his body and the system took him that day. He never went home to his mama. And maybe that's a good thing. Mama was clearly in a bad way. But that kid survived all of those homes, all of that added trauma, and he talks about memories of being physically abused, overmedicated, and blamed and shamed the entire time, and then for him to have the fortitude and the resiliency to graduate from high school and then be homeless the next day. I just found that outrageous.

So, that's something that we work hard on at The Mockingbird Society. We started a national effort for safe housing for foster youth up to age 21. And because of that effort, the Federal Government passed a law, one of the last pieces of legislation that President George W. Bush signed into law. Now, all states are given a Federal Match from the Federal Government if they provide safe housing to foster youth up to age 21. That originated right here with the pilot that The Mockingbird Society successfully advocated for in Washington State, and then it was turned into national legislation. So, we're very proud of that, and especially proud of the youth who testified and worked on the legislation.

Fran: That is awesome, Jim, absolutely awesome, heroic – from you, the humble leader.

Jim: Well, thank you, and I have to say, it was one of the few times that I literally got thrown out of a Senator's office when I brought the idea up.

Fran: That didn't stop you, did it?

Jim: Ha! No. The Senator said, "You're always advocating and giving me a hard time for how we don't take good care of kids under 18 and now you want the state to expand their liability to the kids over 18?" He was furious with me and said, "This meeting's over." Before I got up I asked his assistant, a young assistant who I kind of knew and he happened to be in the office there, so I said, "Hey Bob, how old are you?" And he said, "23." And I said, "Well, where do you live?" And he said, "With my mom and dad." And that was a game changer – even for that legislator to realize that we were not asking for anything for these young people in foster care that isn't the community standard. Particularly during the great recession, there were all kinds of data showing that young people were living back at home, as old as 25 to 30 years old, because they just could not make it on their own.

So, here's another thing that I believe strongly in. We have to look – not at how we treat those kids through the lens of pathology and criminalizing and all of that in terms of behavior, but really – what's the community standard?

And there's another issue that's related to this where we have tried for years to make sure that an attorney represents young people who go into Dependency Court. I don't think most people know that across the nation kids in foster care have regular court hearings, and most of the time kids don't even know there's a court hearing going on. But when they do know, if they go to court, they are frequently the only ones in the courtroom without an attorney. And this Dependency Court is where some of the most important decisions will be made. For example: "Will I get to visit my siblings? Will I get to go home?" One of the things we do in our trainings is we will ask, "How many of you in the room have kids?" Many people raise their hand. And we ask, "How many of you will allow your kid to go into a courtroom without an attorney?" And virtually every hand drops.

Fran: Certainly.

Jim: I think it's pretty much an American standard, certainly a middle-class standard that if my kid's in court, I will take a second mortgage out on the house to make sure she or he is represented by a good attorney. So the community standard is that most of us do not allow our own children to enter a courtroom without legal representation. One of my guiding principles is the community standard for how we treat our own children. That should be the standard of what we provide to children and adolescents in foster care.

Fran: I think of the word legacy when you speak of this accomplishment at the Federal level for that law for all states. That's huge. That's impactful for our quality of life, not just for the youth, but for all of society. I'm also imagining that what it took for you is a story that would fill a book – a book that you could write.

Jim: Well, I've never written a book so I don't know, but I would say it's been an uphill battle, both for changing public perception, and then getting the investment from the State, particularly during the time of the great recession. And I want to say that this Extended Foster Care program is not just about foster youth - it is absolutely a strategy of an even bigger goal to prevent and end youth homelessness.

One of the things that local communities don't always appreciate is when the state discharges youth from foster care it is a burden on the young person, but also for the local community. In Washington State, up to 525 young people every year turn 18 and are at high risk of becoming homeless after foster care. And when they age out of the foster care system, they go to the local communities and become part of the homeless youth population, and often end up incarcerated as a result of engaging in survival behaviors. Yet another example of my previous point about how our "systems of care" often make the problem worse.

We absolutely must get these systems (foster care, juvenile justice, mental health) to stop discharging kids when they know there's really no family or a place to go. Instead they say, "Okay, your time's up, we've done everything we can, you're free to leave." We have to correct this so the local communities can focus their precious few resources on those kids who become homeless because of family conflict or because their sexual identity is such that the family put them out. When systems are discharging youth directly into homelessness it becomes almost overwhelming for the local communities. So we see Extended Foster Care also as a strategy that prevents and ends youth homelessness, specifically for those youth coming out of foster care.

Fran: You know, in the spirit of this book, *The Illusion of Hopelessness*, it caught my attention when I heard your tagline, "Homeless not Hopeless." I see the point you're making about the bigger goal of ending youth homelessness.

> Homeless
> not
> Hopeless

Jim: Yes.

Fran: So back to Mockingbird, what is your business structure in terms of your main organizational focuses?

Jim: Our major program is what we call the Mockingbird Youth Network. And I really do think it can be a national model. We have chapters in six of the major cities across the State of Washington. We co-locate each Chapter with another social service agency in that community that already does much of the adolescent contracts and business relations between the state and foster care. So there is already a building that's a magnet for young people in those communities. In Spokane, for example, the social service agency that we work with has their own shelter right in the building. They have the independent living contracts. So the young people are already coming to that location for services. Each one of those six chapters has three levels of impact.

The first level of impact is – the individual youngster. What are we doing to help that youngster through not so much another counseling experience, but rather a healthy adolescent social enrichment experience? Each chapter typically offers activities toward this goal. The young people talk about how much they appreciate it because they walk in the room where there's a peer group of kids in foster care. So it's not like school or the soccer team where they have to explain things, or as some kids share: "You know, when the car pool drops me off from soccer, I've always had them drop me off a block or two away, so they don't see that I actually live in this big group home." When they come into this chapter meeting they don't have to explain any of that. That's all transcended.

The second level of impact is – the community. So one of the things I tell the young person is, "I am sorry that this crummy stuff happened to you. And yet I still have expectations and confidence that you have something to offer the community." I think these kids are too often given the message that the community needs to be protected from them, rather than kids hearing that they are invited to the table of community as a member and a young leader in this community. So my goal from the beginning has been to invite them to the table of community, not as victims or treatment plans, but rather as young leaders in this social justice movement. Each one of the chapters has adopted a local senior center. One chapter was a kind of graffiti clean-up brigade. They wiped off all the graffiti for the local businesses. It was remarkable how the local business members really flipped the switch on how they viewed these young people. One of our major efforts is to "humanize" these kids to the rest of society. It seems odd to have to do that, but so often people have stereotypes of who these kids are and most of those stereotypes are fear based and media-driven.

The third level of impact is – system reform. So as I tell all these young people, "We're trying to change this system, not only for you today but for that five-year-old child who doesn't even know she's going to be in foster care yet." And it's remarkable to me how, when they hear something like that, you feel the enormity of responsibility that we are sharing with them. They sit up straight and say, "Let's get started." So, it's the sense that they have something to give back. I tell them that really all we do is geared toward system reform. I say, "I hope that your life is stronger and better. I hope that the community recognizes what you have to offer, but in terms of being laser focused and mission driven, our ultimate goal and challenge is to pass legislation and get it implemented for fundamental change, both today and tomorrow in foster care, on the streets, and in the Juvenile Justice System."

We've got to have some way to engage these young people, but not as people who are going to be our future inmates or future welfare recipients. We've got to let them know that they have something to offer, and we're going to make room for them to get that degree and come back and be the next leader in whatever domain or field they choose.

I feel like sometimes the service system is the biggest problem, in that we get so busy about fixing folks instead of really acknowledging that in many ways most of us carry some heavy trauma from childhood or life. Life is hard. That does not mean that anyone needs to be destined to be somebody's client for the rest of their life.

I try and be a mentor around hope. The first piece of legislation I wrote in 1999 was called the Hope Act. And I am very open about the fact that I am living proof that you don't have to be perfect to be loved. I am very blessed with the people around me and there is no way I come close to being perfect. And I think sometimes these kids get a skewed view that they don't have access to quality relationships and a healthy life, and that's the hope I want to give them. With all my efforts to change systems and build quality programs, I'm quite clear: Policies don't change lives, programs don't change lives – *relationships* change lives.

Fran: One of the things, Jim, that stood out for me at the Annual Benefit Luncheon was how you engage the youth. You call forth their creativity, their passion, and their ability to be their own advocate. You offer them opportunities to contribute. You inspire and engage the youth for generating youth-inspired solutions. Please tell us more about that.

Jim: I've been a soccer coach for years and I played sports, and so I really do subscribe to the coaching philosophy as part of my job. One of the things that young people have that no one else has is the real life experience of what it means to go to foster home #25, family #25 with some sense that maybe this time it will work. So the youth-inspired solutions are really a link to that Mockingbird Youth Network that we talked about at the luncheon. There are two major annual events where all the Mockingbird Youth Network and our chapters participate.

One is the Foster Youth and Alumni Leadership Summit ("the Summit"). Our participants discuss ideas throughout the year in their chapters, and then bring their ideas to the Youth Summit. These are ideas that would improve the system based on their experiences(s). We invite them to look at the things "I am" and "we are" facing now, so that if we could fix this, things would be better for kids today and for kids tomorrow. And so they come to this leadership summit and they work hard! We often hear from their foster parents, counselor, etc. how amazed they are that the youngster they know at home is able to rise to this standard of work ethic. We bring consultants and professionals from the different systems, the law school, the schools of social work, lobbyists and legislative assistants together to help the youth think through and refine their ideas and proposals. It's the real deal. The youth are really being challenged to refine ideas so that a legislator could sponsor legislation that Mockingbird would advocate for during the legislative session, with the vision that if passed, the Governor might sign it.

On the final day of the Summit, the youth take their finished proposals and report out to the Washington State Supreme Court Commission on Children in Foster Care ("the Commission). And then those ideas typically show up on our legislative agendas. Extended Foster Care is an example. We've gotten over 25 pieces of legislation passed since we started Mockingbird. Another example is Sibling Visits. Every year at the Summit, youth share about how they are separated from their siblings and want to visit them. As a result of their hard work and advocacy, currently if a sibling visit is cancelled, the social worker has to let the supervisor know, and the supervisor has to document in the file why it was cancelled, and makes a note that the supervisor is aware of it. So we have elevated this issue to where they are conducting the sibling visits more frequently and we think the law has helped push the system in that direction. This is yet another example of how valuable the sibling visits were to the children and youth in foster care, but really not prioritized by the system. Now they are!

One of the pieces of legislation that was really controversial was about the state social worker coming for the monthly inspection of the foster home. In the past, they typically called the foster home anywhere between a couple of days to a week prior to coming to do the inspection. We got a bill passed so that now 10% of all monthly visits have to be unannounced. This was very controversial, as many foster parents thought it was some kind of attack on them and their credibility and some were very offended. They were upset with me. I got hate mail from as far away as Florida. It hit the circuit among foster parents that Jim doesn't trust foster parents, and some felt this legislation was proof of that. It was actually just the opposite, because I also got emails from really great foster parents who said, "You know, as long as it's not a witch hunt from the state, then you can come anytime. There is probably going to be unfolded laundry on the couch and there may even be breakfast still on the table needing to be cleaned up, but the kids are safe. You can come to my house anytime." And that was the philosophy I supported. I have tremendous admiration and respect for our foster parents. They open their homes and their hearts to kids every day, frequently without proper resources. They are true heroes! What helped win over the legislators was when one of our a youngsters said this to the Commission: "When the Health Department is going to inspect a restaurant, do they call three days ahead of time?"

Fran: Ahh, a good point.

Jim: And she added, "And we would like to be as important as any of the items on that menu." So there's an example of an advocacy topic that was presented at a Youth Summit, and we turned that into legislation and got it passed and it is now law.

Fran: That is powerful. And I was thinking – accountability, you know, holding people accountable for promises that they have made.

Jim: That's right, that's exactly right. The interesting thing is, this shows you where kids start in their thinking. The unannounced visit issue actually came up on the first day of the Summit. It started with the young people wanting all foster parents to have psychiatric evaluations and take urine analysis tests.

Their explanation was, "Well that's 'cause whenever they don't know what to do with me, that's what they make me do." I thought that was profound and tied back to my point about only looking at how to fix behavior, rather than looking at communication and asking, "What is going on with you?"

But the other point related to that was, asking the proponents for this law, "What's underneath this idea?" Well, basically some of the youth did talk about how their foster parents were using drugs and drinking too much beer. But what it really came down to was those monthly inspections. And most of what we heard from kids was about when the foster parents get that call and they knew the social worker was coming in three days, the kids would literally say, "My life is hell for those three days. Not only are we cleaning from top to bottom – that part was okay. But then we were told, 'If you tell this social worker that foster daddy drinks too much beer, or that we had this fight; if you tell them what's going on in this home in a real way, you will be homeless. We will kick you out; you will be homeless. You will be a bum like your dad or a whore like your mama.' " We heard the vitriol that kids were experiencing as they geared up for that monthly inspection.

Also we addressed the piece about requesting social workers to not ask kids sensitive questions in front of their foster parents, like "How are things going here?" I mean, it's fine to do that in a general way, but we ask them to take the kid for a walk around the block and let them talk to you, not in the presence of the foster family. Give them that private time.

So there's an example of where the young people experienced something and that bubbled up through the chapter into the Annual Youth Summit, and ultimately became a piece of legislation.

Fran: Whew! That is a powerful story. I am imagining the positive impact for their self-esteem and confidence for the youth to see the difference they are making and that they can make a difference. You mentioned a second annual event for youth engagement. What is that?

Jim: The second annual event that the Mockingbird Youth Network produces is Youth Advocacy Day. Every year during Washington State's legislative session, we have a lobby day. When I first started it I could drive the kids in my vehicle and I'd pick them up along I-5 down to the Capitol and we would have 5 to 10 kids. This last year we had over 250, all wearing The Mockingbird Society's signature orange scarves – all of them laser-focused on the one or two bills we have active at that point in the session – all of them with their notes that they take around to their legislators, whom they've gotten to know before the session started. They drop off notes and have meetings with legislators. We often have a legislative hearing, so kids will actually testify on Extended Foster Care or whatever legislative issues we are supporting at that point. At the last three lobby days we've been thrilled that we've been able to be present to witness the House of Representatives voting on one of our bills while our youth were sitting in the chambers. All you could see were young people with orange scarves watching their bill get passed. It started with their ideas in their chapters.

Fran: Oh my, this brings tears to my eyes. I am so moved.

Jim: Yes, and Fran, I'm a trained therapist. But when a young person really works hard, goes to that meeting when they didn't want to, casts their ideas, tweaks them just enough to where they kind of feel their ego getting bruised, goes through all of those processes – testifying, etc., and then that bill gets passed, nothing changes their perception of what they can accomplish in their life more than something like that.

Fran: I get it; I absolutely get it.

Jim: The pride they feel when they look at me afterward and exclaim: "This is going to help me and that five-year-old child too!"

Again, as a coach giving them the tools and the confidence to take life on, it's very rewarding to watch young people really look at themselves differently, like, "Wow, I never really knew I could do something like this."

Fran: You are generating a hologram of transformational impact from deep within the body, mind, and spirit of the youth you are serving, from the local communities to the national level, and the social service systems, Jim.

Jim: I appreciate that. But I think about what I've done and I don't want to make it seem too special because I want people to know that they can do it too. Rather than getting fixated on blaming and shaming kids, I think what kids learn in the system, unfortunately, is that relying on adults always makes it worse. And they may have learned that even before they went into foster care if they were abused and/or neglected.

But the other thing they learned is a concept from Psychology 101, "Locus of Control". They ask themselves, "Do I believe I can do something to impact the world?" It starts when we are an infant. If we are crying and someone rushes over and changes a soiled diaper or gets us a bottle, we start to learn right then, "Wow, I can make things happen." One of the things that's happened to these young people, survivors of such trauma, is that they come to learn that the only way they can really change things or impact things, is to do what I call, "peeing in the fan and getting everybody wet," which basically means some negative behavior that basically raises the roof and sounds off the alarms. For example, a group of us were having a discussion because one of our youth could not get his social worker to return his call. He was selected to go on an overnight outing with his school and he needed his social worker to sign the consent form. The youth said: "Dang! She won't call me back. I've called a dozen times. I've got to get this form signed." Then another youth spoke up. "I know how to get ahold of my social worker. I always get a call back from my social worker within five minutes." Another youth asked: "Well, how do you do that?" The young man responded, "I just call them and tell them I'm suicidal and I leave my location."

So, I think kids who have experienced abuse and/or neglect learn that their "locus of control" and their power comes from being dysfunctional, in crisis, and that they are someone who needs assistance from someone else. I've tried to expand this notion for these kids by creating opportunities for them to have meaningful involvement in this social justice effort so they experience making the world better for themselves and that five year-old child coming behind them. This has proven a winning strategy to increase the positive power of young people, change the public perceptions of who the youth really are, AND create meaningful system reform.

Fran: And that it's possible.

Jim: Absolutely. That's exactly right. In fact the thing that so many of us, including these young people, will resort to is: "It ain't fair!" And I remind them of what they have learned all too young: "If you want fair, go to Coney Island. Life ain't fair, but you have what it takes to make it better for you and those you care about."

Fran: I also learned at the luncheon that you have founded a revolutionary model for the Foster Care System. Tell us about that.

Jim: One of the other issues I saw as a young therapist was not only were the policies and the budgets messed up and keeping kids stuck, but that we were delivering foster care in a way that met the needs of state government, but did not meet the needs of the kids, birth families, or foster families involved with this system. I had the privilege of growing up with my grandma in the living room, or right next door, virtually all of my life. I think that is where my idea for the extended family model came from. But, again, I really wanted to change not just the policies, but the practice of how we deliver foster care. So I started the Mockingbird Family Model. I started thinking about how I could come up with something that was different and effective. From a place of strength, I asked, "What does any child need to thrive and what does any family need to provide for an environment where a child can thrive?" Particularly one who had some severe difficulties and trauma. That's very different than many of the social service and mental health models that pretty much start with, "How do I fix that kid, how do I address that symptomatology?" I did not want to start there. I wanted to address "What does any child and family need so the kids can do more than survive – they can actually thrive!?"

So the Mockingbird Family Model is based on the Extended Family Theory. We bring six to ten families together. They're all licensed foster families. They each have between one and three foster kids and they live within close geographic proximity. In an urban area, that means they live within 20 minutes of each other. In the rural area, that might mean they live 45 minutes from each other. So they have this micro community and then we introduce another component that we call the Hub Home. The Hub Home is also a licensed foster family, almost always a veteran family, someone who's been doing this for quite some time. The Hub Home then plays the role of grandma or of grandpa in the extended family concept. The Hub Home may have their own kids, but typically they don't. For fidelity and to be true to the model, they have two empty beds in their home and their main job is to provide proactive and reactive support to those other six to ten families.

In the traditional system foster families talk about dreading the honeymoon being over, meaning that the kids came in and for the first week or two, probably things are going to go okay, and then the testing starts. In the Mockingbird Family Model, families talk about, "Can't wait till the honeymoon period gets over, so we can get to the real work." And they can do that because they know they've got not only support of that Hub Home, but of those six to ten families. For example, the Hub Home might call and say, "Hey, it's seven in the morning. We heard you got a new kid last night. When do we get to meet him or her? What kind of support do you need?"

We heard one story recently where the foster parents said, "Well, we thought we were going to get a teenager, but they sent us a four-year-old, so I need four-year-old stuff." So everybody rallies around and gets that.

The Mockingbird Family Model has to have two empty beds in the Hub Home and another fidelity requirement is a monthly meeting. All the families come together. It's a chance for the kids to play and build their relationships, and for the adults to also receive and give peer support to the each other. There's typically a meal at the monthly meeting. There's a training session that goes toward their continuing education credits that they need to retain their foster parent license. And there's just a whole lot of community building. So, it's that proverbial village that Hillary Clinton and the rest of us like to talk about. We've created that and we've created community around kids.

The national retention rate of foster parents is about 50%. In this state alone, we've gone from 6,500 foster homes to about 5,000 in the last year and a half. Sometimes families leave the system for good reason, like they adopted a child, for example. But all too often, we have abused and neglected adults taking care of abused and neglected children. The foster parents talk about the same kind of parallel process and issues that the kids talk about. They can't get a return call from the social worker, they feel isolated, they got a youngster who wanted to go visit their family and the situation broke down so the visit didn't happen. Not only did it feel really sad for the foster parent to witness the pain of the foster child, but all of a sudden the foster parent is the target of the child's emotional outburst, mainly because no one else is around. This takes an enormous toll on foster parents – again the emotional pain they feel seeing their child in pain, but also they are "the last man standing" and took the brunt of it because the child had an emotional meltdown for the next two days. First of all, in the Mockingbird Family Model siblings do not have the same barriers to visitation and, secondly, that foster parent would have the support of the Hub Home family, as well as all the other families in that constellation. This support has resulted in an over 85% caregiver retention rate in MFM constellations.

So what we're getting now with our Mockingbird Family Model is a placement rate, or high stability rate, of 85–90%. This means that kids are not moving around from home to home, school to school. They are stabilizing and have the support of an entire community to making reunification and/or adoption much more likely. Our experience is that our kids run away fewer times than their peers in the traditional Foster Care System. And when they do run, they're gone less time, because they can come home and re-enter through the Hub Home. And that's really what kids tell me about their decision to run away. That it was an impulsive, emotional outburst. They often knew two blocks away that they had made a mistake. Now they can call the Hub Home, which is a healthy relationship they have with another adult(s).

But the real beauty is, in the Mockingbird Family Model they don't have to run in the first place. When they feel the stress or when the family feels the stress, any of them can say,

"Let's call Ms. Degale (Hub Home), let's call Miss Anne, let's call..." whoever the Hub Home person is, and see if you can go and hang out there for the rest of the afternoon or spend the night. So actually kids start to learn, one of the ways to regulate and manage their emotional energy, they now have a safe house, a way to do that. They have another opportunity to strengthen their positive power and locus of control.

> They have another opportunity to strengthen their positive power and locus of control.

In the traditional system, there's no Hub Home, there's no back-up, there's no plan B, so everyone involved has to white knuckle it through the crisis. And sometimes that means, it just overwhelms, overloads, and explodes.

Fran: Oh, that's beautiful. So these statistics, 85-90% are really confirming – validating that your model is working.

Jim: We are working very hard on conducting a major expansion of the Mockingbird Family Model, significantly increasing the number of children, youth, and families being served. We're hoping that by 2016 we will conduct a full evaluation of the model, which should give us the quantitative and qualitative data we need to tell us and the community the true impact we are having through the Mockingbird Family Model.

But the other thing I want to point out is the cost effectiveness. What I hear is, "Oh that Hub Home, that's new money, how do we get that new money." And this is where I do get frustrated at all of the money we spend on foster care and so much of it seems directed toward addressing failings of the traditional model. Instead of changing the service delivery model we focus on the symptoms of the failing system.

Here is one example – if the kids in the Mockingbird Family Model have siblings, they are able to visit each other without the drama of the system trying to coordinate the visit. One of the key symptoms of the failing system is that we frequently separate siblings from each other and often place them in foster homes that are in different parts of the county – or even state – from each other, ensuring the logistics of scheduling any visit between siblings will be more complex and certainly more expensive. Sometimes siblings can't live together due to a court order, if there was some kind of abuse or incest. But mostly the reason siblings cannot live together is that there are too many for one household. So we have sibling groups living in different homes, but in the same constellation. For them to visit each other is much less complex, and again, going back to Locus of Control, "How do I make something important happen? If my behavior is positive I get to call the Hub Home and my sister and I are going to spend the night at the Hub Home Saturday night." How beautiful is that? This is how we motivate in a positive sense – letting youth know that they really can create positive opportunities for themselves through their choices and behaviors.

In the traditional system, because of the lack of foster homes, kids are often split up, living in a different county, maybe on a different side of the state. Because it's not about what's the best bed, what's the best family for this kid, it's often about where there's an open bed. How do we even find a bed for this kid? So in the State of Washington we spend several million dollars a year on sibling visitation. And that's because, if you and I are siblings and we can't be placed near each other, we have different foster families, we have different social workers, we've got to figure out how to get that visitation to happen. And then, at the last minute, if that visitation is going to get cancelled, or even if it does happen, what I hear from foster families is, "Okay, they had the visit and the kid came home and he or she was a mess for three days and I don't want any more visits because that just means my life's crazy for the next three days and that just proves this kid has attachment problems."

For me it's the opposite. If that kid is crying for three days after a sibling visit, that shows me that kid is bonded. That's not an attachment disorder, and for me, that's the voice of being scared about how long it will take to get another visit. In the Mockingbird Family Model, these kids are able to ride their bike to the Hub Home and see each other. So we're very proud of the Mockingbird Family Model. I really do think that we've got to look at how we deliver foster care differently in the 21st century than we did when it all started, which was about fixing kids and changing kids and that sort of thing.

So now, how are we growing kids? How are we helping them get back to their families as quickly as possible when safe? And, if not, then how are we at least giving them a stable childhood? Too many of the kids in care have horrific stories of being picked up at school and informed that they are moving homes, schools, and neighborhoods with virtually no transition time, no good-bye party, often not even an opportunity to get all their belongings from their bedroom. That is how you create kids with attachment problems.

I talked to a youngster the other day that is not living in the Mockingbird Family Model. He was on the basketball team, and he had started kind of a fun relationship with what he thought might be a girlfriend. He had been told that he was on track for adoption by his foster parents. The social worker met him at his school with all of his belongings and a black garbage bag in the car and told him that he's being moved. And he said, "Well, I didn't do anything wrong." I mean, I think they always assume it's their fault. His social worker said, "They've decided they're going to get a divorce and neither one of them can handle you alone and neither one felt like they could talk to you about it."

Fran: Oh my, this is heartbreaking.

Jim: So, he gets in the back of a car and will not return to that same school and is in some shelter somewhere in Seattle, starting all over again.

Fran: That is so sad. What I'm hearing essentially, is that your whole approach to working with the youth and the systems reform is about shifting that mindset from the need for fixing to growing healthy youth and healthy systems.

Jim: That's right, and again I go back to my days as a participant in sports and as a coach, that if all I focus on is fumbling the football, rather than how to hold it and how to protect it and how to get you in a better position when we give you the ball, then all we do is focus on what's wrong and the negative. As simple and silly as that sounds, I think that is where the hope comes. The hope comes from realizing that "I can now carry that ball and I can run and make good yardage in the same way that I can show up on time and they're going to feed me breakfast and they're going to go over my speech one more time and Jim's going to remind me of the Mockingbird Rule," which I remind them of every time we do a public speaking event. And then they're going to go and they're going to do great. And then they're going to get all this support and accolades afterwards. So, I think it's about letting the kids that come in contact with us know that they ought to expect to be viewed as something more than a list of problems to be fixed, and then it's about demonstrating to the rest of the community that this approach works.

Fran: You said something about reminding that youth of the Mockingbird Rule. What is that?

Jim: I have a Mockingbird Rule that I came up with on the fly when I started the organization with those three homeless youth and we got our first opportunity to speak before the city council.

> The Mockingbird Rule is, if you take the task seriously, if you practice, and if you speak from the heart, whatever you do will be perfect for that day.

The Mockingbird Rule is, if you take the task seriously, if you practice, and if you speak from the heart, whatever you do will be perfect for that day.

That's been part of the legacy around here. It's not that you can show up willy-nilly. You have to take it serious. You have to practice! But you don't have to be perfect for it to be successful.

Fran: It's all there. That's beautiful. Jim, let's wrap up with a success story about one of your youth in your program.

Jim: For me it goes back to those three levels of impact. It's a huge success story for the organization to know that in Washington State there are 350 young people in Extended Foster Care right now, which means they're in college or they're in a work environment instead of being on the streets or incarcerated, and because of Extended Foster Care that's happening across the nation.

In terms of individual stories, we've got a bunch of them! We've got young people right here who I met when they were incarcerated and now they're in their first year of community college. But to tell a little bit of a story, last legislative session when we had our lobby day, our Youth Advocacy Day, I was standing there and it was cold and blustery, but someone tapped me on my shoulder and I turned around and looked and there was this young woman who started with us at age 15. She began participating in our Tacoma Chapter and was so shy at that time, that we first just said, "No, you don't have to talk, just you being in the room is powerful and positive." And after awhile she felt comfortable enough to write something and hand it over and someone else would read it for her. And she just continued to grow to where she did testify in front of a legislative committee and later she became a Chapter Leader. And by the time she aged out at 18, she was a phenomenal young woman and young leader. Well here she is, tapping me on the shoulder and she is an intern for one of the state senators.

Fran: Oh, my gosh! That's terrific!

Jim: She had been to a Youth Advocacy Day four or five times as a youngster. But now she is there, coming down from her fancy professional office to assure me that she had been talking to the senator, and that she has the senator's vote in line for us. But it was just so heartwarming to see one of our young people up in the deep halls of the legislative buildings and working with the senator. I mean, I teared up on this one. I could do it right now, if you knew this young woman from the beginning when she came to us a very shy young girl.

And then a few minutes later I got another tap on my shoulder and here's a young woman – same thing – she was with us for so many years and now she is a youth counselor at a Youth Shelter. She was the staff person that brought half a dozen kids from her program to the Youth Advocacy Day. Now she's a professional staff person. So that was just remarkable. And then about an hour later we were in the House of Representatives and they were voting on the passing of the latest version of Extended Foster Care.

Fran: Awesome. Heartwarming. It makes all those long hours and hard work worthwhile, doesn't it?

Jim: Indeed! So to me that's what it's about, having these wins, and I've said it from the beginning, my deepest joy would be that as I transition out at some point there'd be alumni at foster care, leading this organization.

Fran: Oh, that's easy to see. You know, your stories that you've shared. Those youth have grown up with The Mockingbird Society and now they're giving back in the system, making a positive difference in the system. That's easy to see.

What is your vision for the future?

Jim: Well, I often say that when I'm an old goat sitting on a park bench, I would love to know that The Mockingbird Society is still this little engine that could, continuing to be laser focused and mission driven around elevating the voice of youth to advocate for improving foster care and ending youth homelessness. It is my greatest vision that this organization can survive and sustain beyond me and continue to be a force, making sure that young people's voices are heard, and that the system is looking at young people and families – not as something to fix, but as customers who need some service, and with that service they will be able to get to the next best place.

Fran: And I hear that you're not attached to the specific forms that journey takes, but that this organization is laser-focused – and mission driven – on ending youth homelessness.

Jim: You got it!

Fran: And certainly you have been successful with a launch and a growth and, at this point in time, have a momentum going that's impacting on a national level. So, it's easy to see, Jim, that this vision will be realized and will continue.

Jim: Yes, that's the hope and prayer. That's the belief.

Theories don't change lives – relationships do.

Programs don't create nurturing homes – dedicated adults do.

> "Systems don't raise
> healthy children –
> families and
> communities do."
>
> Jim Theofelis

Section Five: Resources

COACHES – VOLUNTEER OR PAID?

Pros with Volunteers: Volunteer coaches do their work because of an intrinsic motivation. Where a trusting relationship with a client is important, this seems to be highly valued by the youth. Feedback from youth is that they interpret this to mean that the coach really cares about them – that someone is willing to help them without getting paid for it.

A fully trained, accredited coach can offer part of their time as a volunteer, working with only one youth-at-risk at a time, for example. In this way, the coaches can support themselves financially with their full-time private coaching business. This also supports the coach with their well-being and life balance.

Cons with Volunteers: The difference in the quality of service with volunteers may introduce inconsistencies in the quality of overall organizational service. Turnover may be greater with volunteers, running the risks of less long-term commitment and higher costs of administration, recruitment, and training.

Pros with Paid Staff: The organization attracts professional coaches who can afford to commit to full-time and/or long-term commitment, providing a more stable workforce.

Cons with Paid Staff: There is higher overhead in payroll costs. Also, this jeopardizes trust for some youth who perceive the coach is being paid to work with them.

Competencies and Characteristics of a Qualified Coach

Screening of coaches is important. One way to ensure qualification of the coach is to require accreditation by the International Coach Federation:

ACC (Accredited Certified Coach), PCC (Professional Certified Coach), or the highest level, MCC (Master Certified Coach). Accredited Coaches have completed rigorous classroom training, supervision, and examinations, as well as a scope of experience working with clients. They have satisfactorily demonstrated proficiency with the required eleven Core Competencies, which are identifiable ways that coaching competencies are made actionable and visible. The following is a brief overview. For the complete list, go to: *http://www.coachfederation.org/icfcredentials/core-competencies/*.

General Category	Core Competency	Brief description
A. Setting the Foundation		
	1. Meeting ethical guidelines and professional standards	Understanding of coaching ethics and standards and ability to apply them appropriately in all coaching situations
	2. Establishing the coaching agreement	Ability to establish clarity and alignment with the client
B. Co-creating the Relationship		
	3. Establishing trust and intimacy with the client	Ability to create a safe, supportive environment that produces ongoing mutual respect and trust
	4. Coaching presence	Ability to be fully conscious and create spontaneous relationship with the client, employing a style that is open, flexible, and confident

C. Communicating Effectively		
	5. Active Listening	Ability to focus completely on what the client is saying and is not saying, to understand the meaning of what is said in the context of the client's desires, and to support the client's self-expression
	6. Powerful Questions	Ability to ask questions that reveal the information needed for maximum benefit to the coaching relationship and the client
	7. Direct Communication	Ability to communicate effectively during coaching sessions, and to use language that has the greatest positive impact on the client

D. Facilitating learning and results		
	8. Creating Awareness	Ability to integrate and accurately evaluate multiple sources of information, and to make interpretations that help the client to gain awareness and thereby achieve agreed-upon results
	9. Designing Actions	Ability to create with the client opportunities for ongoing learning, during coaching and in work/life situations, and for taking new actions that will most effectively lead to agreed-upon coaching results
	10. Planning and Goal Setting	Ability to develop and maintain an effective coaching plan with the client
	11. Managing Progress and Accountability	Ability to hold attention on what is important for the client, and to leave responsibility with the client to take action

The highest priority competencies for a coach working with youth-at-risk are:

- Adherence to ethical standards
- Caring and compassionate
- Ability to build and sustain trust and rapport
- Active listening
- Ability to hold the client capable, creative, and resourceful.

Most successful programs offer specialized training for the coaches, focused on the specifics and uniqueness of their target population (age, substance abuse, juvenile court, etc.).

Grace is granted for individual coaching styles, based on their personality and innate strengths. Coaches are successful with their clients when they can express and function in their individual styles, as long as the Coach adheres to the guiding principles and philosophy of coaching.

CARE/SUPPORT FOR THE COACH

It is critical for the success of any youth program that the coach is provided with programs, relationships, and services that support their ongoing well-being. The work is stressful at best. A healthy, grounded, centered coach can provide a healthier environment for a client than someone who is worn out, stressed out, or burned out.

Monthly meetings allow coaches to exchange experiences and ideas; offer support to one another; share successes, tips and practices; and offer extra training, techniques, and tools, and reinforce building, refining, and augmenting skills and use of tools.

The coach works one-on-one with his or her own coach. Whether the organization provides for a personal coach for the volunteer or paid coach, or the coach provides their own, it is critical that a coach has their own safe space and committed support for their self-care, self-management, and well-being.

One of the most challenging aspects of working with youth is the ability to be there fully with patience and without judgment, especially when the client experiences setbacks. This requires a level of emotional maturity that comes naturally for some and more difficult for others to maintain. This is a place where the peer meetings and the coach's coach can be a sounding board, and support for clearing concerns and releasing tensions.

PROGRAM DESIGN

Best practice for a highly successful youth program is a multifaceted program that includes:

- 1:1 relationship with a coach; this is a long-term relationship built on safety and trust
- Regular small group peer sessions; these are community building for youth, where they can share their experiences and know that they are not alone; these can be guided group discussions or group coaching sessions
- Community service initiative that has the youth engaged in making contributions to others (community garden, food bank, legislature, community centers, etc.)
- Programs for learning and practicing life skills and/or work skills

Selection of Coach/Client Match

Attention to a best "chemistry" match for coach and client enhances the effectiveness of the coach-client relationship.

It is ideal that the client gets to choose their coach. Offering choice reinforces a message to the youth that they have choice, which is an important and consistent element of the coaching approach throughout the program. Providing choice also demonstrates respect, and reinforces building of trust and rapport.

LENGTH OF PROGRAM INTERVENTION

The variables, of course, for the length of time a youth will remain in a coaching program are numerous. Primarily this determination would be based on the specific objectives of the program and the nature of the funding.

Ideally, the longer, the better! With short-term interventions, there is a tendency to rush people through the program to meet funding quotas or timelines. Not every youth in the program will be able to sustain the short burst of a fire hose of a comprehensive six-month program.

Best practice is fewer youth in the program over a longer period of time – the *quality versus quantity* approach – supporting them to be successful when they are ready to engage with the world. Target: 0% recidivism.

PARENTS – INVOLVE THEM OR NOT?

Some individual coaches involve the parents and some don't. It depends on the coach's individual style and the types of issues their clients are dealing with.

Some organizations involve the parents and some don't. Often-times it's not even possible. If it is possible to involve the parents in your program, the ideal is to help the parents cultivate a safe supportive environment at home for their youth.

TOOLS

The following are tools mentioned by some of the contributors.

- **Wheel of Life** – This is a picture of a wheel with 8–10 spokes. Each section is labeled with aspects of living. For example: work, health, family, friends, money, home/housing, significant relationship, spirituality. Or it's a blank wheel, and the coach invites the client to fill in his/her own categories.

Then the client establishes a measure of their level of satisfaction in each of those areas, on a scale of 1–100%. This establishes a baseline that can be revisited periodically over time to measure progress.

At this point it is also an opportunity for coaching the client with questions, such as:

o As you look at the overall picture, what do you notice?

o What area do you want to focus on to raise your level of satisfaction?

o What is one action you could take this week that would raise your level of satisfaction?

Now the coach will support the client in following through and helping the client to learn how to hold themselves accountable.

- **Goal Setting** – The elements of a goal setting process for the coach can include:
  o Helping the client name a goal they want to achieve
  o Checking on the client's level of commitment or motivation
  o Facilitating the client in designing one, two, or three *simple and doable* actions they *can* take
  o Explore possible barriers
  o Coach to clear the barriers
  o Co-create with the client a tracking or reporting system
  o Follow up with each step
  o Acknowledge the client for their efforts and the qualities of their character they are demonstrating (i.e.: courage, responsibility, strength, resilience)
  o Celebrate the smallest successes and the big ones!

- **Life Planning** – This is a tool for designing a future vision and how to begin living it. A coach will typically help the client design their Life Plan and coach them over a period of time with a focus on learning how to hold their vision clearly in mind, like a guiding light, and how to make choices day-to-day in alignment with their values. Elements of a Life Planning process can include:
  o Vision statement
  o Purpose and/or mission statement
  o Values
  o Guiding Principles
  o Life goals with target dates
  o Specific action steps

MEASURE PROGRESS

The question is, "How well are we positively impacting the quality of the lives of youth in our program, the community, and society at large, and how do we measure our impact?" Organizations take responsibility for showing themselves, supporters, and funders successful returns on their investments, whether emotional or financial. The challenge is how to do that effectively.

The biggest gains from coaching are typically the intangible benefits for clients, driven by shifts in thinking and behavior. The most visible of these benefits are enhanced communication skills, better ability to relate to self and others, and stronger decision-making and creative problem solving skills, as well as improved self-management. These can be difficult to quantify, as these vary with every individual.

Subjective approaches can include:

- Narratives – Individual client success stories that are communicated through websites or newsletters. Coaches track and report their client's goal-setting and achievements, positive changes in behaviors, risks taken, strengths and capacities enhanced, growth in self-esteem and self-confidence, etc. Success stories become an asset for the culture of the organization.

- Goal achievement – coaches support clients in setting small doable steps to achieve goals. Goals and actions are tracked on a tracking sheet. These small achievements are reported – and celebrated!

- Wheel of Life tool – At the beginning of the relationship, the client measures their own level of satisfaction, establishing a baseline in key areas of their life. This is revisited periodically together with the coach to track progress. This is a visual tool that also gives the client a way to see their own progress.

Objective approaches can include:

- Number of clients who satisfactorily complete the Program
- Number of clients who do not return to jail/prison
- Number of clients who show up for their 1:1 appointments and group meetings
- Number of clients who become employed
- Number of clients who gain stable housing

Roster of Contributors

I hold these contributors with my highest regard for their vision, passion, compassion, commitment, and perseverance. If you have been touched by these stories and you feel called to contribute to this transformational approach for changing our social systems, please contact these heroes in the trenches, and ask them what you can do. There are a thousand ways to make a difference. No action is too small:

- Learn and model the coaching approach in your life and work.
- Take the coaching approach with the youth in your sphere of influence.
- Volunteer your time with youth at community service organizations.
- Contribute positive political influence.
- Contribute money.
- Share this book with others.

CONTRIBUTORS

David Lockett
djlockett@rogers.com
(416) 256-0726

Jason Wittman
jason@theparentscoach.com
(818) 980-2929

Jim Theofelis, MC
jim@mockingbirdsociety.org
(206) 407-2131

Jodi Sleeper-Triplett
jodi@jstcoach.com

Joe Cotton
jcotton@stjames-cathedral.org
(206) 264-2082

Jude Delsoin
jmdelsoin@gmail.com

June Maresca Justice
June.Maresca@ocj-cjo.ca
(905) 456-4935

Kate Sharpe
kate.sharpe@sympatico.ca
(416) 463-2023

Mark Demos
mark.demos@corp-dna.com
(425) 492-4300

Morgan Rich
explore@playhuge.com
(503) 475-8294

Reuel Hunt
reuel@coachingkids.org
(303) 734-0444

Shawn Harding
shawnharding@gmail.com
(647) 786-1808

Spark Inside
Baillie Aaron, Founder and Director
www.sparkinside.org
exec@sparkinside.org
+44 (0)78 6975 8756

Steven Cessario
contact@teenagesons.com
(860) 338-9856

Wendy Fortune
wfortune@fortunelifemanagement.com
(416) 953-8120

Will Manos
willmanos333@gmail.com
(416) 873-6337

CANADA

PACT Urban Peace Program

Empowering and supporting youth through LifeSkills Community Service Programs and our award-winning LifePlan Coaching for high risk youth in conflict with the law. Transformative early prevention programs with remarkable results!

312 Brooke Ave
Toronto, ON M5M 2L3

Ben Marshall - 416 656-8824
ben@pactprogram.ca
http://pactprogram.ca/

Macdonald-Laurier Institute - True North in Canadian Public Policy

MLI is a nonpartisan, independent national public policy think tank based in Ottawa that focuses on the full range of issues that fall under the jurisdiction of the federal government.

8 York Street, Suite 200
Ottawa, Ontario, Canada K1N 5S6

(613) 482-8327
www.MacdonaldLaurier.ca

ENGLAND AND WALES

Ministry of Justice

Youth Justice Board Executive Summary 2014
www.gov.uk/government/publications/youth-justice-statistics

Clinks

Supporting voluntary organizations that work with offenders
and their families.

59 Carter Lane
London EC4V 5AQ

Tel: 0207 248 3538
info@clinks.org
http://clinks.org/

The Howard League

For Penal Reform – Less Crime, Safer Communities, Fewer
People in Prison

1 Ardleigh Road
London, N1 4HS

Tel: +44 (0) 207 249 7373
info@howardleague.org
www.howardleague.org/

Spark Inside

Non-profit; coaching young people involved in the criminal justice system.

Baillie Aaron, Executive Director

York House (5th floor)
207-221 Pentonville Road
London N1 9UZ

+44 (0) 203 468 0706
info@sparkinside.org
exec@sparkinside.org
www.sparkinside.org

USA

ACT for Youth Center of Excellence
Bronfenbrenner Center for Translational Research
Beebe Hall
Cornell University
Ithaca, NY 14853

Phone: (607) 255-7736
Fax: (607) 255-8562
act4youth@cornell.ed

Homeboy Industries

Homeboy Industries serves high-risk, formerly gang-involved men and women with a continuum of free services and programs, and operates seven social enterprises that serve as job-training sites

130 W. Bruno St.
Los Angeles, CA 90012

(323) 526-1254

info@homeboyindustries.org
www.homeboyindustries.org

National Coalition for the Homeless

Bringing America Home - a national network of people who are currently experiencing or who have experienced homelessness, activists and advocates, community-based and faith-based service providers, and others committed to a single mission: To prevent and end homelessness while ensuring the immediate needs of those experiencing homelessness are met and their civil rights protected.

2201 P St NW
Washington, DC 20037

(202) 462-4822
info@nationalhomeless.org
http://www.nationalhomeless.org

The National Network for Youth

Working to create a system of agencies, people, and resources to champion the needs of homeless and runaway youth, to ensure that opportunities for growth and development be available to youth everywhere.

741 8th Street, SE
Washington, DC 20003

(202) 783-7949
www.nn4youth.org

Touch Point Connection

Supporting Adolescent Success and Life Readiness Through Coaching – Is It Possible?

Touch Point Connection, a 501(c)(3) organization, has completed its five-year pilot program.

Our Vision: Through the power of coaching, Touch Point Connection envisions youth who become self-reliant, confident, and responsible, and whose contributions and choices as engaged citizens positively impact the quality of life for them and their community.

For information, contact
HAdams@touchpointconnection.org
www.touchpointconnection.org

Youth Mentoring Connection

Empower Youth. Inspire Communities. Change Everything. Dedicated to strengthening the youth of our communities with a very unique approach – by seeing their gifts and acknowledging their wounds.

1818 S. Western Ave. Ste. 505
Los Angeles, CA 90006

Tony LoRe
CEO & Founder

(323) 731-8080
tony@youthmentoring.org
www.youthmentoring.org

The Mockingbird Society

The Mockingbird Society trains youth who have been homeless or in foster care to become their own best advocates. Our youth then help change policies and perceptions that stand in the way of every child having a safe and stable home. We also support families and advocate for innovation in the way our society delivers care. Together, our programs offer youth-inspired solutions, build powerful coalitions, and ensure public support for every child's right to a healthy future.

2100 24th Ave S, Suite 240
Seattle, WA 98144

(206) 323-KIDS (5437)
LinkedIn Group: Life Coaching Teens & Young Adults
Administrator: Sandi Lindgren, PhD, MSW
sandi@isupportyouth.com

Articles

"Urban Peace – How Do We Get There?" 7-6-14

http://tinyurl.com/urbanpeace

Co-Founder David Lockett also developed and has run a program for nearly 20 years that embraces society's toughest, hardcore juvenile criminals and gives them the tools to turn their lives around. It's called the PACT LifePlan and Coaching Program and its guiding principle is the idea that if we help young people avoid a lifetime of crime, everybody wins.

Contact Diane Dimond at www.DianeDimond.com or Diane@DianeDimond.com

"After Recession, More Young Adults Are Living on Street," by Susan Sulney, New York Times, 12-18-12.

http://tinyurl.com/homelessyoungadults

"National Network for Youth Recommendations for System Enhancements toward Ending Youth Homelessness," 9-25-12.

http://tinyurl.com/nn4ypdf

"Homeless Youth," published by the National Coalition for the Homeless, June, 2008.

http://www.nationalhomeless.org/factsheets

This fact sheet discusses the dimensions, causes, and consequences of homelessness among youth. An overview of program and policy issues and a list of resources for further study are also provided.

Books

Tattoos on the Heart, the Power of Boundless Compassion, Gregory Boyle, Founder of Homeboy Industries, Free Press 2010

Shattered Lives, Children Who Live With Courage and Dignity, Camila Batmanghelidjh, Founder of Kids Company, Jessica Kingsley Publishers 2006

Empowering Youth with ADHD, Your Guide to coaching Adolescents, Jodi Sleeper-Triplett, Specialty Press 2010

The Street Shrink Chronicles, Jason Wittman, Artful Graphics Press 2010

Launch Your Life: 5 Secrets to Knowing What You Want in Your Teens, College Years, and Early Career, Morgan Rich, 2008

The Art and Science of coaching Parents, Caron B. Goode, Ed.D. NCC, Inspired Living International 2007

The DNA Code, Mark R. Demos, Lightening Source-Ingram House, 2012

The Struggle to Be Strong, Edited by Al Desetta, Sybil Wolin, Free Spirit Publishing, 2000

Youth At Risk: A Canadian Overview, John A. Winterdyke and Russell Smandych, Oxford University Press 2012

Youth at Risk: A Prevention Resource for Counselors, Teachers, and Parents, David Capuzzi and Douglas R. Gross, Prentice Hall Paperback, American Counseling Association Paper 2008

Quotes – Teens and Hope

TEENS

We're so used to seeing adolescence as a problem. But the more we learn about what really makes this period unique, the more adolescence starts to seem like a highly functional, even adaptive period. It's exactly what you'd need to do – the thing you have to do then. National Geographic, The New Science of the Teenage Brain

Our youth want less adult contact if that contact treats them like boys. They want more adult contact that treats them like young men. Tired as they are of the former, they are hungry for the latter. Michael Gurian, *The Wonder of Boys*

In scientific terms, teenagers can be a pain in the ass. But they are quite possibly the most fully, crucially adaptive human beings around. National Geographic, *The New Science Of the Teenage Brain*

HOPE

I believe that imagination is stronger than knowledge. That myth is more potent than history. That dreams are more powerful than facts. That hope always triumphs over experience. Robert Fulghum

I find hope in the darkest of days, and focus in the brightest. I do not judge the universe. Dalai Lama

We must accept finite disappointment, but never lose infinite hope. Martin Luther King, Jr.

No matter how dark the moment, love and hope are always possible. George Chakiris

You may not always have a comfortable life, and you will not always be able to solve all of the world's problems at once, but don't ever underestimate the importance you can have, because history has shown us that courage can be contagious and hope can take on a life of its own. Michelle Obama.

Life is meaningless only if we allow it to be. Each of us has the power to give life meaning, to make our time and our bodies and our words into instruments of love and hope. Tom Head

Where there is no vision, there is no hope. George Washington Carver

Hope is the key for transforming your pain to perseverance. Patrick Snow

It takes courage to grow up and become who you are. E.E. Cummings

Darkness cannot drive out darkness; only light can do that. Hate cannot drive out hate; only love can do that. Martin Luther King, Jr.

He who has hope has everything. Arabian Proverb

The wound is the place where the light enters you. Rumi

Never doubt that a small group of thoughtful, committed citizens can change the world. Indeed, it is the only thing that ever has. Margaret Mead

The greatest thing about man is his ability to transcend himself, his ancestry, and his environment to become what he dreams of being. Tully C. Knoles

As human beings, our greatness lies not so much in being able to remake the world... as in being able to remake ourselves. Mahatma Gandhi

We change our behavior when the pain of staying the same becomes greater than the pain of changing. Consequences give us the pain that motivates us to change. Henry Cloud

Be of service. Whether you make yourself available to a friend or co-worker, or you make time every month to do volunteer work, there is nothing that harvests more of a feeling of empowerment than being of service to someone in need. Gillian Anderson

Nobody can go back and start a new beginning, but anyone can start today and make a new ending. Maria Robinson

You are the master of your destiny. You can influence, direct and control your own environment. You can make your life what you want it to be. Napoleon Hill

Systemic poverty can reduce people's choices and diminish their spirit. However, poverty doesn't define individuals, nor limit their potential. We believe that each person has within them a reserve of skills, interests, abilities, values, and hopes for self-development. We call this human capital. The Prosperity Agenda www.theprosperityagenda.org

And so the voices at the margins get heard and the circle of compassion widens. Souls feeling their worth, refusing to forget that we belong to each other. No bullet can pierce this. Gregory Boyle, Tattoos on the Heart

233

After dealing with a particularly exasperating homie named Sharkey, I switch my strategy and decide to catch him in the act of doing the right thing. I can see I have been too harsh and exacting with him, and he is, after all, trying the best he can. I tell him how heroic he is and how the courage he now exhibits in transforming his life far surpasses the hollow "bravery" of his barrio past. I tell him that he is a giant among men. I mean it. Sharkey seems to be thrown off balance by all this and silently stares at me. Then he says, "Damn, G... I'm gonna tattoo that on my heart." Gregory Boyle

Hafiz

There is a Beautiful Creature
Living in a hole you have dug.
So at night
I set fruit and grains
And little pots of wine and milk
Beside your soft earthen mounds,
And I often sing.
But still, my dear,
You do not come out.
I have fallen in love with Someone
Who hides inside you.
We should talk about this problem –
Otherwise, I will never leave you alone.
by Hafiz

This poem by Hafiz has a beautiful line: "I have fallen in love with someone who hides inside you." It expresses the essence of the work we do at Youth Mentoring Connection. We realize that hiding inside every confused, angry, shy, sad, or braggadocios child is a gifted soul that came into this world to contribute from their genius. When a mentor comes into the life of a young person, they are affirming that something beautiful is hiding inside of that child. In fact, the poem describes the process of mentoring for at-risk youth. **It is a process of consistently showing up and offering sustenance in the way of caring, listening, deep**

conversation, and guidance to help young people to begin to climb out of some of the holes they have dug. This requires the ability to "see" beyond their behaviors and attitudes and into the goodness that we all possess.

In our efforts to help keep the spirit of "seeing" alive we have adopted a Zulu word as our customary greeting whenever we get together in program. The word is "sawubona" and it means "I see you." It speaks to the necessity in each of us to have our gifts affirmed and to know that we are valued, by each other and by our community.

Tony LoRe, CEO & Founder
Youth Mentoring Connection

Gratitude

This book would not exist without the love, support, and contributions of the people I will name here, and the multitude of family, friends, and colleagues who aren't even aware of how they have affected my ability to learn, grow, and hold true to this Vision and Mission.

Thank you, dear editors. Each of you contributed enormous heart-centered generosity of your time, energy, expertise, belief in the message, and possibility for profound social change:

- Linda Lane, who helped me launch this project and build momentum with her project planning, structure, and editorial expertise.
- Elizabeth Burroughs-Heineman, who showed up like an angel on the ground, editing with her highest integrity for the true voice of each contributor.
- MJ Schwader, who pulled it all together and got it to market, honoring his commitment for excellence.

Thank you to those of you who provided manuscript feedback that helped me make key decisions at important choice points along the way:

- My Author MasterMind buddies: Ron Rael, Toolie Garner, and Emiko Hori. Our mutual support and creative synergy is pure magic.
- Diana Dollar – Your straight-forward, honest feedback was the catalyst for shifting my approach to better alignment with the empowerment message.
- Berry Zimmerman – You walk the talk as a "Go-Giver." I am deeply grateful for your contributions to my learning and growth, personally and professionally.
- Howie Adams – Thank you for championing this project every step of the way, especially the finishing touches.

Thank you Jude Spacks for your deep listening and coaching facilitation that helped me clear those internal limiting voices and unleash my vision, passion, and self-confidence.

Thank you Adria Trowhill and Steve Miko, for your trust and belief in me, and giving me the space to honor Craig in this way.

Thank you Catalina Chaux and Ben Marshall, for providing direct access to your resources at PACT. I appreciate your support in keeping Craig's legacy alive.

Fran Fisher
January 2015

About the Author

FRAN FISHER, MASTER CERTIFIED COACH

 **Fran** is a Master Certified Coach (MCC), visionary leader, international speaker, and published author. She specializes in providing mentoring for coaches, and coaching services for small business owners, executives, and collaborative teams.

Recipient of The Lifetime Achievement Award 2012 by the ICF Chapter of Washington State, Fran is recognized internationally as one of the pioneers and champions for coaching. She served as a founding International Coach Federation, ICF, Executive Board member, and co-chair of the Ethics and Standards Committee, responsible for developing the Credentialing Programs for aspiring coaches and training schools. Fran was the first Executive Director of the Association for Coach Training Organizations, ACTO. She is currently serving as an ICF Credentialing Assessor.

Fran's passion is helping people liberate their authentic power and manifest their highest visions. She specializes in facilitating a transformational approach for blending the art of visioning with the structure of strategic planning and intuitive listening to empower her clients for greater success and fulfillment.

In 1991, Fran founded the Living Your Vision® (LYV) process for empowering individuals in transforming their visions into reality. In 1997, Fran founded the Academy for Coach Training, one of the first International Coach Federation (ICF) accredited schools. In 2005, shifting her focus to private practice, and more writing and speaking, Fran sold the ACT and LYV businesses and their associated trademarks to I & AM, LLC dba inviteCHANGE.